Braving the Minnesota Wilderness

The Soderbergs:
Sweden to early Sandstone and
the Gunflint Trail

Joyce Leddy

ISBN-13: 979-8-8693-9454-5

Printed in the United States

10 9 8 7 6 5 4 3 2 1

Produced By
Northern Wilds Media, Inc.
Grand Marais, MN
www.northernwilds.com

Braving the Minnesota Wilderness

*The Soderbergs:
Sweden to early Sandstone and
the Gunflint Trail*

Joyce Leddy

Dedication

To
Eva Soderberg Cleaver,
my mother,
who taught me to appreciate
all the wonders of Minnesota's Northwoods.

Preface

When I was a young child in the 1940s I would spend part of each summer living with my mother's parents—the Soderbergs. Both of my grandparents emigrated from Sweden in the late 1800s. They met in Sandstone, Minnesota where they were early settlers.

I was an only child, and not having many playmates in Sandstone, I learned to sit quietly and politely whenever my grandmother's friends came to visit. As they sipped coffee, which was strained through eggshells in the Swedish way, and sampled freshly baked cinnamon rolls out of my grandmother's wood-burning stove, I became fascinated by the incredible stories of survival these women shared.

In 1950, when my grandparents became elderly and infirm, they moved in with my family on the northwest side of Chicago. Emma Flood Soderberg was part of our household for two years until her death in 1952. Charles Soderberg lived with us until he passed on in 1955. Gratefully, even in Chicago, the stories never stopped. In fact, they also included tales of my uncles' experiences on the Gunflint Trail.

The Soderbergs were not unique. They were struggling Swedish immigrants who came to Minnesota to find a new life. They worked extremely hard for very little. While pursuing the American dream, like all early settlers, they faced unforeseen challenges and many losses. They probably never attained their goals. Yet in retrospect, now that I have white hair, I realize perhaps sometimes success needs to be judged by different standards. It took enormous courage to leave behind family, friends, and a beloved homeland to establish a new life in an untamed wilderness.

Life on the Minnesota frontier was a great time for the adventurous. The land offered extraordinary beauty and abundant resources for the pioneer. However, these assets were often overshadowed by a harsh terrain and violent, unpredictable weather. During difficult times, it took considerable self-sacrifice, fortitude, and skill just to keep one's family together.

My grandfather, Charles Soderberg, had both the adventurer and pioneer spirit. No matter what adversity he faced, he remained in awe of the forests and lakes of Minnesota. In fact, he ignited such a love of this land that three of his children eventually moved even farther north—deeper into the wilderness of the early Gunflint Trail. There they practiced the well-honed skills of survival, which he taught.

In 2010, my husband and I took a trip to Sweden with the hope that we would be able to locate my grandparents' farms – one in the province of Småland, the other in Dalsland. The Swedish Institute in Vaxjo was extremely helpful, and we were successful in our search. Interestingly, while at the institute, surveying the various displays about the Swedes who had left for America, we were surprised to learn that the institute was interested in hearing what happened to those immigrants.

As I recall, it was voiced that when families left the hardships of Sweden, often they did not fare much better. If anything, their lives became more difficult and perhaps even tragic. I subsequently learned that about one-fifth of Swedish immigrants returned to Sweden. That statistic surprised me. Although certainly my childhood had been filled with first-person accounts of great privation and tragedy, I also heard of the many joys and opportunities a pioneer life offered. I wrote this book to chronicle the Soderberg's unbridled spirit, and to honor all of Minnesota's courageous settlers who, in the face of profound adversity, found the faith and determination to carry on.

The Soderberg Family

I. SWEDEN

Dalsland

John Flood (Jan Peter Jonasson), b. 1852 Högsäter; d. 1905, Sandstone, MN. Emigrated to America in April 1887.

Eva Eriksdotter Flood, b. 1843 Högsäter; d. 1930, Sandstone, MN. Emigrated with five children in September 1887.

Children:
>   Oskar (Oscar) b. 1874 d. ?
>   Johan (John) b. 1876 d. 1955
>   Helen (Anna Helena) b. 1878 d. 1887
>   Emma b. 1881 d. 1952
>   Sissy (Amanda Kristina) b. 1883 d. 1968
>   Alvina b. 1891, MN d. 1914

Smaland

Charles Soderberg (Carl Johan Pettersson), b. 1871 Tävelsäs; d. 1955, Duluth, MN Emigrated in 1892.

II. SANDSTONE, MINNESOTA

Charles Soderberg married Emma Flood in 1899, Duluth, MN

Children:
>   Violet b. 1899 d. 1942
>   Floyd b. 1900 d. 1974
>   Helen b. 1904 (daughter: Andrene Heinecke Tuck, Mpls) d. 2004
>   Carl b. 1906 (daughter: Carlene Soderberg Krumpack) d. 1969
>   Eva b. 1911 (daughter: Joyce Cleaver Leddy) d. 1998

III. THE GUNFLINT TRAIL and GRAND MARAIS, MINNESOTA

Floyd Soderberg, Built the first cabin on Birch Lake, 1947

Carl Soderberg, Built the "Soderberg Cabins" on Poplar Lake, 1945
m. Elinor Pusner

Eva Soderberg, Purchased Trail Service Center on Poplar Lake, 1963
m. George Cleaver

Table of Contents

1

SWEDEN

Sweden is the largest of the Scandinavian countries. There are nearly 270,000 islands off its coasts and close to one hundred thousand lakes within its interior. Ancient, vast boreal forests cover half of the nation. Its principal cities lie on the coasts, and its Arctic north, like Norway, can poetically be called, "The land of the midnight sun."

Even with this great richness and beauty, in the late nineteenth and early twentieth century, approximately 1.3 million Swedes left for the United States. In fact, census figures from 1870-1900 show that a large number of those Swedes came to Minnesota, including both of my grandparents—Emma Flood and Charles Soderberg.

Historically, by the middle of the nineteenth century, "Sweden was in the throes of a national population crisis—the small country's population had doubled from 1750-1850, and was still growing. Tillable land became more and more scarce, and famine swept the nation, killing twenty two out of every one thousand Swedes. Emigration regulations were eased and the 1860s saw a massive movement of Swedes fleeing their homeland;"[1]

Famine and a shortage of farmland were not the only reasons there was a great surge of emigration. Other factors were:

1. Religious persecution—the government was tied to the Swedish Lutheran State Church.
2. Lack of social mobility.
3. Mandatory military service.
4. Reports that the American Midwest was a paradise with religious and political freedom.

Charles Soderberg (1871-1955)

The Soderberg story needs to begin with the fact that my grandfather's real name was not "Charles Soderberg." His Swedish given name was Carl Johan Pettersson. When Charles arrived in America, an immigration agent warned him that with a common surname like Pettersson he would have great difficulty getting mail. Therefore, it was decided that he would take the name of his farm in Sweden—Södergård," which means "South Farm." Either my grandfather's English was impossible to understand or the agent took some liberties. Södergård was recorded as "Soderberg," and the family has carried that name forward ever since.

Småland

Charles was born in 1871 in the village of Stenslanda, Tavelsas Parish in the province of Småland, which is located in southern Sweden, about 119 miles from the large port city of Göteborg (Gothenburg).

Unfortunately, little is known about my grandfather's life in Småland. I was told that he grew up on a farm and was the youngest child in a family of five children. I do not know whether his family owned the farm or were merely tenant farmers. Sadly, my grandfather's mother, who was crippled, died when he was nine years old.

Several years ago, my husband and I were able to locate my grandfather's farm in Småland. This was a very sentimental trip for me as I vividly remember Grandpa Charlie describing his farmland—how it was full of rocks, but had wonderful forests and lakes nearby. When I finally stood on his land, I couldn't help but note several large boulders near what is now a private home. In a poignant moment, I realized that as a young boy Charles must have played on those very rocks.

Yet, what was even more heartwarming and remarkable to me was our drive through a nearby forest. The wooded terrain was filled with firs, pines, and birch trees. There were red cabins and lakes, and clusters of blue lupine graced the side the road. To my surprise, this forest was nearly identical to the Gunflint Trail area outside of Grand Marais, Minnesota, where we have a cabin/home. It made me understand why the forests and lakes in Minnesota meant so much to Charles, and why later in his life he encouraged his children to embrace the wilderness of the Gunflint Trail.

Having visited the Södergård farm in Småland, it would seem that as a young boy, Charles had the best of both worlds. Not only did he have the opportunity to learn the skills of farming, but of hunting, fishing, and

Södergård.

trapping as well. Although Charles worked alongside his father in the fields, most of all he loved the woods. Even when he was elderly and infirm, his eyes would light up whenever he would talk about the forests and lakes in Sweden. He said during the winter, when the lakes were frozen, he would ice skate two miles to school every day.

Beväringen—Military Service Requirements

It is believed that Charles emigrated from Sweden in 1892 at the age of twenty-one. That was the same year his father died. Charles left behind two sisters and one brother. I was told that my grandfather left Sweden because he did not want to be in the military. Up to the time of his emigration, the government had relied upon a universal conscription system called "Beväringen," whereby all able-bodied men fit for military service had to undergo a minimum military training in the armed forces. Since its establishment in 1812, the requirements for military training underwent various changes. By 1892, a new Army Act was adopted where service time was increased.

Charles Left Sweden Without a Certificate

Our family still has some unanswered questions about my grandfather's emigration. According to the Swedish Institute in Växjö, Charles was missing from the census in 1892. This would have labeled him as someone

Högsäter farm today.

"without a certificate," and prevented him from purchasing a boat ticket from Sweden to America. Although we do not know where Charles was living between 1892-1895, we understand he left for America from Copenhagen. Census records show Charles Soderberg arrived in Sandstone, Minnesota in December 1895.

Emma Flood Soderberg (1881-1952)—Dahlsland

My grandmother, Emma Flood (Soderberg)'s parents were Eva Eriksdotter and Jan Flod (Jan Peter Jonasson). In 1886, the year before their emigration to America, the Flods and their five children were listed as living on a farm with Jan's mother in rural Brasäter Sodra, near the town of Högsäter in the province of Dalsland, which lies on the Norwegian border (about ninety-three miles north of the port city of Gothenburg). In my family research, I discovered the name Flod was a "soldier name," which was changed to "Flood" in America.

Patronymic Names

During the nineteenth century, Swedes followed the "patronymic" naming system where last names were generally derived from the father's given name (first name) with the addition of the suffix "son" meaning son or "dotter" daughter. To the avoid confusion of many common names, a military company commander usually "christened" a new soldier with a

Eva Eriksdotter Flod.

Jan Flod.

military name. When Emma's father, Jan Jonasson, became a soldier, he was given the name "Flod" which means "river" in Swedish.

In 1901, the Name Adoption Act was passed, which abolished patronymic practices. Afterwards, many families adopted names from nature —e.g., Berg (mountain), Dahl (valley)—or a place of origin, or military-oriented names.

Torps

Since my grandmother Emma Soderberg's father was a military man, I was surprised to learn that just before their emigration, the Flod family was living on a farm in Högsäter. Perhaps I can speculate that difficulties in Sweden forced the Flods to join their extended family on one of their parents' farms. On the other hand, it is also possible that the Flod family had been granted what was called a "soldier farm." In some parts of Sweden, small farms—called "torps"—were given to a soldier at the end of his military service. However, the soldier and his family were usually required to move after the discharge (or death) of the soldier.

I imagine the Flods' decision to emigrate to America in 1887 was based on many of the same reasons other Swedes fled Sweden that year. However, it is sobering to note that during the mid- nineteenth century there were auctions of poor children and infirm elderly.

Through obituaries, I learned that several members of Eva Eriksdotter Flod's family (the Eriksons) had preceded them to America. I believe the Flods were forced to delay their emigration because of family circumstances. According to the 1886 Swedish census, Jan's mother died one year before they left. Those records also show that Eva Flod gave birth to an unnamed child who died in 1886.

2

Leaving for America

My grandmother, Emma Flood (Soderberg), left Sweden with her family in 1887 when she was six years old. My grandfather, Charles Soderberg, emigrated by himself about five years later (1892) at the age of twenty-one. Emma and Charles met in Sandstone, Minnesota, where they were early pioneers. Charles was ten years older than Emma, and they married in Duluth in 1899.

Jan Flod (Emma Soderberg's Father)

In 1887, Emma's parents, Jan and Eva Flod, made plans to emigrate to America with their five children. It was decided that Jan would emigrate first. Perhaps Jan wanted to test the waters in America before making such a life-changing commitment. Yet, more likely, he needed to earn enough money to pay for the rest of the family's passage. On April 22, 1887, he sailed on the steamship Juno from Gothenburg, Sweden, to Hull, England. He listed his destination as St. Paul, Minnesota. It appears he planned to join his wife Eva's relatives (the Eriksons) in Grantsburg, Wisconsin, which lies just over the Minnesota border near Pine City.

Gothenburg and Sillgaten Street

Like Jan Flod, more than 80 percent of Swedish emigrants began their journey to America from the port city of Gothenburg. This bustling city was where one could find temporary lodging while arranging transatlantic passage. Third-class travelers could find cheap rooms on a lively street called Sillgatan—Herring Street—which was nicknamed thus for how emigrants were tightly packed together in hotels.

Sillgatan was a short street—only two-thirds of a mile long. Yet, this little street offered a grand passageway to the custom house pier where small steamers (feeder ships) took emigrants to a British port, like Hull, located on the east coast of England.

After emigrants finalized their travel arrangements, they usually were drawn to explore Sillgatan and other nearby streets. Although Sillgatan was lined with shabby buildings, many flashy window displays enticed emigrants to purchase goods which were claimed to be necessary during their first few weeks in America—e.g., city clothing, tools, and guidebooks.

Sillgatan Street was an exciting place to stay. It carried a wild, carnival-like atmosphere, especially when ships arrived or departed from the "American Pier." It was a place of merriment, but also danger. There were magicians, acrobats, colorful signs, and banners. One could seek a gypsy fortune teller, or buy candy for the children in an open-air market. However, there were also saloons, cafes, prostitutes, watch peddlers, and con men. Oftentimes, travel funds were squandered.

In 1881, during the month of May, nearly nine thousand emigrants sailed on from Gothenburg to Hull, England. After this two-day voyage, emigrants boarded a train and traveled another five hours to a larger coastal city, such as Liverpool, where transatlantic steamships would finalize their journey. It was during this long train ride where indignities began. A third-class passenger had no access to water or restrooms.

Eva Flod and the Children

Jan Flod must have fared well after his arrival in Grantsburg. Five months later he was able to send for the rest of the family. I'm sure Emma Soderberg's mother, Eva, received this news with great happiness. Yet, it must have also been frightening for her to contemplate traveling across an ocean alone with five children. In fact, just to travel from rural Högsäter to a large city like Gothenburg would have been daunting.

Once in Gothenburg, Eva needed to arrange passage for their transatlantic crossing. This process required navigating a list of governmental technicalities. Before departure, an emigrant was required to present a certificate of change of address from their home parish (a Flyttbetyg). This was to be written out by the home parish pastor (hemförsamlingen).

The certificate included the name, address, and profession from which the emigrant moved and to which parish the emigrant was transferring. Information on vaccinations and general social behavior was also included. The agencies, in turn, had to submit passenger lists.

In addition to filling out the proper forms, Eva would have also had to cope with making all the necessary purchases for the journey.[7] Until 1885, it was important for an emigrant to buy a straw mattress to keep from sleeping directly on the boards of the ship's designated bunk beds. Although transatlantic ships provided passengers with food, they were advised to bring a tin cup, knife, fork, and spoon.

The Gothenburg Tree

Even though Gothenburg represented an auspicious time for Eva Flod, I can't help but share an amusing story that has become part of my family's oral history. As I mentioned, Eva was traveling alone with five children. They were: Oscar (thirteen), John (eleven), Helen (nine), my grandmother Emma (Soderberg) (six), and Christine (four).

According to the story, after they arrived in Gothenburg, Eva realized that she would have to stand in long lines to present her documentation to secure passage. Most likely it would take all day. Eva didn't know how she could possibly manage this with five young children in tow. She reasoned that if she left the children behind by themselves, they would get into trouble or wander away. Her solution would not have pleased the child authorities today. Eva found a very long rope and tied the children together under a tree.

I love how my cousin Andrene Tuck chronicled this story for her young grandchildren. She wrote, "It was a very long day for the children, and they waited and waited and waited. And even though everyone got hungry, they had to wait some more. I am sure it was very hard for the children to be so far away from home, tied together with a rope, sitting under a tree in a strange big city, separated from their mother." (Truthfully, I would think thirteen-year-old Oscar must have felt embarrassed to be lashed together with his younger brother and sisters).

Andrene went on to write, "In the afternoon, one nice man came by and said, 'Have you children had anything to eat today?' And when they said, 'No,' he went away and later came back with a bag of rolls and some milk. That made the children feel a lot better. However, then it got dark and they began to fill with fear. But happily, mother Eva came back just as she promised, carrying the tickets and a great big smile."

Although Emma Flood (Soderberg), was only six years old when her family left Sweden, she never forgot the Gothenburg tree or the terrible Atlantic crossing she and her family endured in order to come to America. Eva and her five children set sail on September 5, 1887, for what was to be a two-week voyage. Since the Flod family, like so many other emigrants, only had enough money to pay for the lowest class of ticket—stowage—they were relegated to a small, crowded, horribly unsanitary area in the bottom of the ship.

Tragedy at Sea

"In most of the emigrant ships, space was very restricted, as most ship owners wished to carry as many passengers as they could possibly accommodate, it was common to see five hundred or one thousand passengers crowded into the steerage (third class passengers). Each wooden bunk was six ft. long by six ft. wide and a passenger was entitled to the use of one quarter of such a bunk. The berths were usually arranged in two or three tiers, with four people to each tier. The advertisements all boasted of the extra space available between decks, but many passengers found that they rarely had enough room to enable them to stand in comfort. Unscrupulous agents often put more passengers aboard than the regulations allowed. Ninety percent of the vessels did not have a surgeon on board. ... Seasickness was always a problem, but cholera and typhus were the killers." [7]

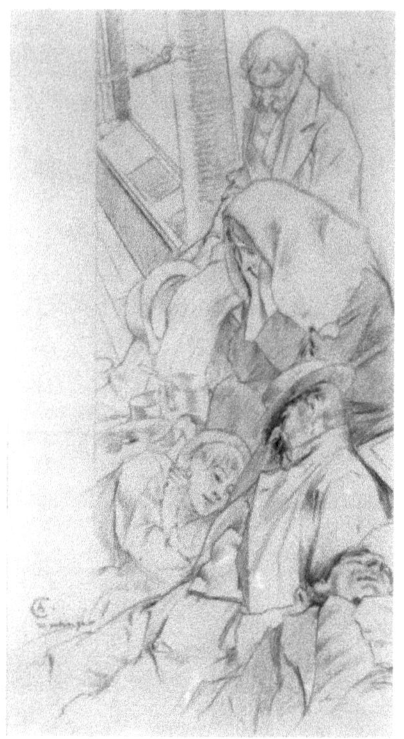

Steerage. | Castaigne, J. André, 1898, from The Library of Congress

Unfortunately, Eva and the children faced a very rough crossing with seasickness and disease. My grandmother told me everyone in the family except nine-year-old Helen became terribly ill. They were so sick they couldn't leave their beds for most of the crossing. While the family suffered, little Helen acted like an angel and nursed them nearly all the way to America. Tragically, just before they reached the new land, when everyone was recovering, Helen fell ill and died. She was buried at sea.

3

America at Last

Arrival at Port

According to the Statue of Liberty-Ellis Island Foundation, prior to 1890, individual states rather than the federal government regulated immigration into the United States. Consequently, in 1887, after Eva Flod's ship landed in one of the major ports—New York, Boston, Philadelphia, or Quebec—her family would not have faced a long immigration process. The immigration station at that time, "Castle Island," was only used to screen those planning to settle in the state of New York.

Once on land, Eva and her four remaining children were still weak from illness and grief-stricken over the death of Helen. Yet, they did not have the luxury of rest or self-pity. Eva had to arrange for transportation to the Midwest.

When the Erie Canal was completed in October 1825, immigrants were able to travel by boat up the Hudson and Mohawk Rivers to Buffalo and the Great Lakes. About five years later, in 1830, train travel became available in the United States. In the beginning, it was quite slow—it could take up to five weeks to reach Minnesota. However, when the Flod family traveled west, train travel took considerably less time. In fact, the railroad line from Rush City, Minnesota, to Grantsburg, Wisconsin, was completed in 1884. I assume Eva and the children were able to travel from their port of entry to Wisconsin entirely by train.

At this point, I should mention that since my grandfather, Charles Soderberg, arrived in America at least five years later than my grandmother, he would have faced a different immigration process. Because the great wave of immigration of the 1890s lasted for thirty-five years, immigration policies changed. Typically, if Charles's steamship docked in New York Harbor in 1892, as a third-class passenger he would have boarded a ferry to Ellis Island for a detailed inspection. (First- and second-class passengers only received cursory inspections aboard the ship. It was believed that the affluent passengers would be less likely to have medical or legal problems.)

At Ellis Island, if an immigrant's papers were in order and they were found to be in reasonably good health, the inspection process lasted three to five hours. Contagious diseases and concern that the individual would likely become a public charge or an illegal contract laborer were the reasons some people were excluded from entry.

Grantsburg, Wisconsin

The township of Grantsburg, Wisconsin, made application to incorporate as a village in 1886, one year before Jan and Eva Flod arrived from Sweden. At that time, the census showed a population of 311 people. The town included three stores, a hotel, two blacksmith shops, a saloon, two churches, and a school. There were also two sawmills, one shingle mill, and a gristmill.

Even though this small community had formed into a village, I surmise that when Jan Flod arrived, the surrounding area would still have been considered a frontier—part of the rapidly changing wilderness. Jan must have been grateful to join Eva Erikson's family in Grantsburg, as they helped him find work, acclimate to his new surroundings, and set up a temporary home.

The Dirt Floor

Unfortunately, after an exhausted and grieving Eva finally joined her husband, it was not a joyful occasion. According to family lore, the new home she expected to find had only one room and a dirt floor. Eva could not help but show her disappointment. After such a long, arduous, and tragic journey, all Eva could do was kneel down on that dirt floor and cry. Eva did not cry for long, however. She was a strong woman of deep religious faith. Filled with a brave heart and the resilient spirit of a true pioneer, Eva decided to stand tall and not look back.

"The Children's Blizzard"

Probably one of the hardest challenges for any northern pioneer was the threat of winter. It didn't matter if you chose to live on the prairie or in a forest; winter storms could be deadly. Even the so-called "hardy Swedes" could not have been prepared for weather conditions like these.

According to statistics, winters in Gothenburg, Sweden, are cool, humid, and windy, with daytime averages between thirty-four to thirty-nine degrees Fahrenheit. Nighttime temperatures range between twenty-five and twenty-eight degrees Fahrenheit. During most winter months, there are only two or three snowy days in Gothenburg. This is a far cry from the subzero temperatures and heavy snowfall that are part of a normal winter in northern Minnesota.

When the Flod family arrived from Sweden in October/November of 1887, they were about to face one of the most harrowing, deadliest winter storms in the history of the upper Midwest. According to reports, the winter of 1887–1888 had been "ferocious and unrelenting." There were ice storms, snowstorms, high winds, and subzero temperatures. On January 12, residents thought they had finally found relief, as that morning they awakened to a "gentle reprieve."

Unfortunately, the early settlers did not know that the Army Signal Corps had issued a cold wave warning the previous night. A dynamic blizzard, now known as the "children's blizzard," was racing across Montana and northern Colorado. This storm caught many settlers by surprise. Tragically, the result was a great loss of life. Most victims were children trying to get home from school or adults working on large farms.

The storm was so severe that it covered 780 miles in seventeen hours. Some accounts say that temperatures fell nearly one hundred degrees in just twenty-four hours. The plains were hit the hardest. Much of North Dakota reported forty below temperatures all day, with high winds and heavy snows that were blinding.

Newspapers in Minnesota, Nebraska, Iowa, and the Dakota territories later estimated that between 250 to 300 people died that weekend. The storm was far reaching. "Much of the press coverage also indicated that most of Minnesota, as well as the surrounding states, felt the wrath of the storm."[10]

Minnesota

Although Eva Flod's family, the Eriksons, found Grantsburg to be the perfect place to put down roots, the Flods only stayed in Grantsburg for one year. I'm not sure of the exact reason why they left, but I know many small towns and farms were just beginning to be established in Wisconsin and Minnesota. The Flods were eager to become landowners, and Jan had an entrepreneurial spirit. Eva and Jan saw special promise in the small Minnesota village of Sandstone. It was only about seventy miles north of Grantsburg.

In many ways, Minnesota was ideal for the pioneer. Its natural resources were plentiful. Minnesota lakes and rivers offered fresh water for drinking; its forests offered good timber for building homes; its prairies had rich soil for farmland; and its wildlife provided an abundance of food for the table.

Ecologically, the reason for the variety of these resources is that four biomes (ecosystems) converge in Minnesota—the coniferous forest, the deciduous forest, the aspen parklands, and the prairies grassland.

A Bit of History

The earliest known settlers came to Minnesota during the last glacial period while tracking game. They were followed by the Anishinaabe, the Dakota, and other native inhabitants. Some believe Norsemen may have explored the area in the fourteenth century. A slab of sandstone inscribed with medieval Germanic script (the Kensington Stone) was discovered on farmland in west-central Minnesota.

In the seventeenth century, French explorers came to Minnesota in search of the Northwest Passage. Also during that century, French fur traders, known as the voyageurs, established the first settlement. Other European settlers who were heading west began to arrive during the nineteenth century.

On May 11, 1858, Minnesota became the thirty-second state. Its Homestead Act in 1862 facilitated land claims by new settlers, and as railroad lines extended across the state, the farming and logging economy was established.

4

Sandstone, Minnesota

Before 1885, Sandstone, Minnesota, was a rugged, undeveloped land home to a few lumberjacks, hunters, trappers, and farmers. The Ojibwe called the area "Asinikaaning," which means "at the quarrying place." Native Americans who lived in villages near the St. Croix River, Rutledge, or Mille Lacs Lake came through the area to hunt, fish, and pick berries. The early residents eventually named the village Sandstone for the rocks found in the quarries on the bluffs of the Kettle River.

William H. Grant Sr., a St. Paul attorney, owned land along the Kettle River that carried extensive sandstone deposits. Realizing this land's economic potential, he opened the Kettle River quarries in the summer of 1885. A little more than a year later, after the quarry was up and running, and Sandstone's first railroad was organized (the Kettle River Railroad Company, [KRRC]), "The KRRC tracks stretched a distance of four miles from the bluff of the Kettle River connecting the quarry with the St. Paul & Duluth Railroad Company rails located west of Sandstone."[12]

After the first sandstone was quarried, the little settlement began to grow. It attracted quarry workers, lumberjacks, and river hogs (drivers). With two saloons, the area was not without its uncivilized settlers. According to town historian Mark Robey, young Sandstone characteristically "saw many a roughhouse and a good many vicious characters."[12]

No doubt my grandmother Emma (Soderberg)'s father, now known as John Flood, heard about the quarry while living in Grantsburg and moved to Sandstone because he foresaw the area's possibilities. It didn't take long before John established himself in business and was able to build a permanent home for Eva—a house with more than one room and a dirt floor.

1889, a year after the Floods arrived, Sandstone incorporated as a village. At this point, besides saloons, Sandstone had a hotel, a bank, mercantile stores, a meat market, a blacksmith shop, laundry, a barbershop, and more than fifty homes.

The eventual success of the quarry in Sandstone offered a new source for jobs in Minnesota. Since quarry workers needed a place to live, the Floods decided to make their new home a boarding house. Within a short time, John opened a saloon and a meat market as well.

The Boarding House

John and Eva Flood's home was located at 430 First Street, within the main village of Sandstone. The white house was beautifully situated on the south hill above the road to the sandstone quarry and the Kettle River. Since there was a great demand for lodging by single men who were working at the sandstone quarry or one of the other local businesses, I'm sure the house was large enough to include several boarders.

Most likely the Flood's boarding house was much like those found in early Minnesota mining towns. Those boarding houses offered temporary lodging, along with three meals a day. Typically, the lodger was given access to a clean sleeping room on the second floor and to a common dining room and sitting room on the main floor. (Usually, the family lived in the other part of the main floor area.) After supper, lodgers liked to spend time visiting, smoking, and playing cards. For the men who still had families in Europe, it was especially enjoyable to have children around.

Men who worked long, twelve-hour days were given a large breakfast in the morning and a late dinner at night. They were also provided a noon meal in a "lunch bucket," which they carried to work. I'm sure all of the Flood family members played a part in making the boarding house a comfortable home that ran smoothly every day. As I recall, outside of consuming endless cups of coffee, my mother's family never sat down—hard physical labor was their mantra for success in life.

Early Life in Sandstone

The family grew to love their new life in Sandstone. In fact, it was hard to feel like a foreigner when so many people in their little town spoke Swedish, and Minnesota's terrain of forests and lakes was similar to Sweden. The early pioneers enjoyed talking about the "old country" and the hardships they faced when they began their new life. Once in school, the Flood children learned to speak English, and it wasn't long before they became as American as everyone else.

I do not know how long my grandmother, Emma Flood (Soderberg), went to school. My cousin, Andrene, believes that she only had a third grade education; yet, I have a letter written by Emma that shows both beautiful cursive handwriting and an excellent use of English and grammar. Whether Emma attended school past third grade or not, I'm sure she began helping her mother with the boarding house as a young girl.

In 1891, Eva and John welcomed another child—a daughter named Alvina. She was born when Eva was forty-eight years old. Now, the Flood family once again consisted of seven members. John Flood must have been a bit of a mover and shaker in town, as the same year Alvina was born, he was elected as a trustee on the city council.

For the most part, families in early Sandstone were self-sufficient. Hunting was common, as wild game—moose, deer, bear, and grouse—were nearby and plentiful. The family garden and local farms provided fresh fruit and vegetables during summer months and enough extra produce to be used for storing or canning for the winter. Since Minnesota winters were long and severe, with temperatures often plummeting to forty degrees below zero, food preservation was essential. Potatoes, beets, rutabagas, and carrots were stored in the root cellar.

The Flood children, like their friends, had a long list of daily chores, including making bread, collecting eggs from the hens, carrying heavy buckets of water from a pump in the backyard, milking the cow, and feeding all the animals. It was also necessary for the chickens to have their feathers plucked before they could be roasted. Wood had to be chopped and dried for the stove, which was used both for cooking and to keep warm in the winter. Outhouses, chamber pots, and kerosene lights were part of a pioneer's everyday life. (Electricity came to downtown Minneapolis in 1882, but it was not until 1908 that the Kettle River Power Company was organized and able to supply electric service to the Sandstone Area. Surprisingly, by 1940, only thirty percent of farms in Minnesota had electricity.)

The good news for young Emma was that some of her chores could be fun. In the summer, groups of friends and families joined together to explore the countryside and pick berries. They often brought picnics along for these outings. The children loved going barefoot all summer, even though this was just a way to preserve shoes. Since Kettle River was close to their home, the Flood children found plenty of opportunity to swim.

My grandmother, Emma, said that when there was enough time, the children would make up their own games. Emma had a rag doll, which she made from pieces of cloth that her mother had left over from sewing. Emma and her sister Christine (Sissy) would also string old buttons and make necklaces. Nothing went to waste. The clothes were always mended, shortened, and lengthened, and were handed down from one child to the next. When the clothes were really worn, they were torn up and used as rags for cleaning, or cut into strips and made into rugs. Even during the last years of her life, I remember how my grandmother would tear up all my old woolen skirts to make beautiful rugs.

"The Shared Dress"

Another story from my family's oral history relates to the Flood sisters, my grandmother Emma (nine years old) and Christine (Sissy, seven years old) during their early years in Sandstone. Since the girls were only two years apart in age and about the same size, they were forced to share clothes. Unfortunately, they only had one good dress between them. As a result, the sisters would alternate weeks to wear that good dress to Sunday School.

A really important and exciting time for the family was when a fair/carnival came to town. Since there wasn't a lot of entertainment for children in early Sandstone, this event meant a lot to Emma and Christine. However, having only one good dress posed a problem for the sisters.

To keep things equal, it was decided that Christine, the younger sister, could wear the dress in the morning to attend the fair. In the afternoon, Emma would have her turn with both the dress and the fair. As the story goes, Christine had so much fun at the fair she conveniently forgot to come home. As a result, Emma missed the entire fair. The next year, as a compensation, their mother Eva made sure Emma got to stay at the fair the entire day.

Kidnapped

The Flood brothers, John and Oscar, were older than their sisters, but also only two years apart in age. According to my cousin Andrene, when John and Oscar, were in their early teens, they gained permission from their parents to help a man they casually knew with a small job in Minneapolis/St. Paul. This job would only require them to be away from Sandstone for a few days.

When the boys did not return home after a considerable time, the family became very concerned. Their father, John Sr., asked a friend who was travelling to the cities to investigate the where-abouts of his sons and try to find out what happened to them.

As it turned out, young Oscar and John were found working like mules. They were being forced to carry heavy jugs of water all day long. They later told their father that it was such difficult labor, that when one boy got tired, he would sit on the shoulders of the other. Gratefully, the boys were found, rescued, and brought safely home.

Of course, those were the days when there were no child labor laws. It was not unusual to see young children working full time under horrible conditions. According to a study about child labor in U.S. history, the University of Iowa Labor Center reported that forms of child labor, including indentured servitude and child slavery, have existed throughout American history. In urban areas, children were preferred because they were more manageable, cheaper, and less likely to strike. The man who kidnapped or "borrowed" John and Oscar had not reckoned upon a caring father.

The Lumber and Fur Industry

When Minnesota became a state in 1858, its grasslands and prairies appeared to stretch endlessly into the western horizon, while its vast forests, teeming with towering and majestic pines, seemed to cover the sky. Unbelievably, two hundred years after European Americans moved to Minnesota, only about 0.3 percent of the natural prairie remained, and the forests had shrunk by more than half. Along with these vanishing lands, countless numbers of wildlife were killed.

Whether it was the result of ignorance or greed, the surge of white settlers changed Minnesota's landscape. Unfortunately, the early settlers thought the bountifulness of Minnesota's resources had no end. Certainly, good land and an abundance of wildlife is key to survival on a new frontier; however, once it was realized that the land, water, and animals could also provide a livelihood, self-interest prevailed. The early economic growth in Minnesota was based upon fur trading, logging, milling, and farming.

There was a great demand for white pine in America. After the great eastern forests were depleted of pine, logging companies were forced to seek new forests. Minnesota met that need. White pine was considered the king of the logging industry, and in the 1800s, some of Minnesota's white pines reached a height of two hundred feet and measured six feet across. Loggers loved working with these pines as they were easy to mill and cut into wood. They also floated in the rivers like cork.

By the mid-1800s, Minnesota's logging operations were in full swing, and with the arrival of railroads, new markets were opened for logging. Eventually, steam power became a boon. It allowed logging companies to have an easier and deeper reach into the dense forests. As a result, logging left behind great swathes of barren landscape, which many believed were the perfect solution for farmers looking for land. The old adage "the plow follows the axe" rang true. Yet, no one warned unsuspecting farmers that the soil was thin, acidic, and poor in nutrients; nor about the amount of backbreaking toil needed to remove stumps and rocks from this now denuded land.

By the 1850s, "professional market hunting" became a thriving industry, and uncontrolled hunting and trapping decimated Minnesota's wildlife population. In fact, it became a slaughter. An English visitor to St. Paul in 1864 ascribed the prosperity of the town to the fur trade. He said, "Every other shop is a furrier. The streets are redolent in hides—wolf, fox, bear, mink, wildcat … seen dangling from windows."[16]

By the 1900s, millions of flocks of passenger pigeons had been killed, which brought the species to the point of extinction. Also, the large numbers of buffalo that roamed Minnesota prairies had nearly vanished.

5

The Great Hinckley Fire

When early settlers arrived in Sandstone, Northern Pine County was covered by grand forests, thick with white, Norway, and jack pine. Unfortunately, with the growth of the timber industry, "Hundreds of lumberjacks soon converged upon the forests, and trees fell by the thousands." In fact, in the 1860s, "665,000 of the county's 906,366 acres were forested and provided prime timber for enterprising lumber companies..."[17]

Sadly, woodsmen often left behind a tangled mass of debris. Over time, the slashings of broken saplings, branches, twigs, stumps, and pine needles baked and dried in the hot summer sun. It was inevitable that careless logging would be followed by fire.

Residents Unprepared

Sandstone was one of six villages destroyed by a catastrophic "firestorm" that began on Saturday, September 1, 1894 between the hours of 2:00 p.m. and 4:00 p.m. Today that "firestorm" is known as the Great Hinckley Fire.

A "firestorm" is a great rarity—an atmospheric phenomenon which is the result of a combination of temperature inversion, trapped gases, and downward rushing air that creates a vortex or a tornado of flames. On that fateful September day, conditions were perfect for two fire systems to converge into one roaring inferno.

People were practically helpless when the storm's concentrated fury unleashed a roaring wall of fire four and a half miles high. It raged towards the small lumber town of Hinckley and other unsuspecting communities, with winds estimated to be seventy-five to one hundred miles per hour and with temperatures of two thousand degrees F. Within minutes, the Great Hinckley Fire consumed everything in its path.

The fire leveled the towns of Hinckley, Mission Creek, Pokegema, Miller (Groningen), Sandstone, and Partridge (Askov). "Over 300,000 acres of forests, and millions of dollars of property were gone in one afternoon."[12] Before the fire died out, it claimed over 400 lives in Hinckley alone. About 80 people perished in the Sandstone area.

A firestorm is not a wildfire. The Hinckley Fire Museum uses some historical comparisons to emphasize the might and speed of this kind of fire. It points out that one of the last devastating "firestorms" in history was caused by the 1945 nuclear bomb explosion in Hiroshima, Japan. In comparing speed, the raging Pagami Creek wildfire in the Minnesota Boundary Waters in 2011 took nine weeks to burn 93,000 acres; yet the 1894 Hinckley firestorm destroyed 307,000 acres in only four short hours.

Early pioneers were aware of the danger of forest fires and knew that these could be caused by lightning strikes, sparks from a train, or by farmers as they cleared their lands. The Hinckley Fire Department felt well prepared. It had nineteen volunteer firemen, a new fire engine, hose cart, and firehouse; "They were positive they could conquer any fire that threatened Hinckley."[17] However, the firestorm that raged through Hinckley that day defied anyone's preparedness or description.

Fire—Everywhere

As children, my cousin, Andrene, and I would always ask our grandmother, Emma Flood Soderberg, to tell us the story of the Sandstone fire. Since Emma survived the fire, no matter how many times we heard the story, her first-hand account would have us sitting on the edge of our seats. In fact, Emma often took us on picnics to the Sandstone Cemetery where, after lunch, she would point out the graves of her young childhood friends who died in the fire. Emma didn't care if we were only children; she left none of the horror and shocking details out.

Although I was quite young and do not remember these accounts as clearly as Andrene, I do remember the effect the fire had on my grandmother's life. Even though Emma was a smart and witty woman, she never overcame her fear of fire. One stormy night when I was about five, I remember my grandmother dragging me out of bed to join her in the living room where she pulled back the drapes and had me keep watch with her looking for lightning strikes.

There have been several books written about the Great Hinckley Fire and many personal accounts recorded. They all describe the summer of 1894 as extremely hot and dry. In the forested regions of northern Minnesota, Wisconsin, and Michigan, fires had flared off and on all summer. The skies over the Great Lakes had been hazy with smoke, and at times created hazardous shipping conditions on Lakes Superior, Michigan, and Huron.

In a book about the history of Sandstone, Matthew Bullis was interviewed about the conditions in Sandstone during the summer of the fire. He said, "June started being dry. July was worse, (with) smoke now starting. August was drier and smokier. Sometimes (one) could not see a block away. Nights got so bad that windows had to be closed in order to be able to breathe...Day after day, no rain, hot sun, smoke."[12]

Bullis went on to say that at night the fires could be seen all around, but they were not considered dangerous. He recalled that the morning of Saturday, September 1, dawned smokier than ever and the sky grew darker and darker. By 11:00 a.m., it was necessary to put the lights on. Gust Gjertson remarked that by 4 pm, it was as dark as night. He exclaimed, "Then the wind and flames came. It sounded like a tornado....big pieces of timber came flying like balls of fire, would strike a house, go completely through it, and the house would explode into flames. The whole country side was an inferno."[12]

Although the Sandstone train station had a telegraph, there was no public warning system. The alarm only spread from neighbor to neighbor and from friend to friend. Families and local fire departments were totally unprepared for this kind of fire and were forced to make life or death decisions within moments.

A Harrowing Escape

In 1989—one hundred years after the Great Hinckley Fire—the account of my family's experience during the fire was also published in *Sandstone, the Quarry City*. The account was written by James Larsen, the grandson of "Sissy," Christine Flood (Berg), my grandmother Emma Soderberg's younger sister. The following is that account. I have taken the liberty of making a few corrections (in italics) regarding my grandmother Emma and the Flood's youngest daughter, Alvina.

"Christine, *Emma*, her two older brothers, John Jr., Oscar, and younger sister, *Alvina*, lived with their parents, John and Eva Flood, in a big white house on the south hill above the road to Sandstone's quarry and the Kettle River at 430 First Street.

"The summer of 1894 had been hot and dry. Christine was eleven years old that September and was looking forward to the first day of school. Christine's mother had sewed new dresses for the young Christine, and, like any eleven-year-old, she could hardly wait to wear them to school. On that terrible September day, it was hot and dark. Smoke filled the skies and by early afternoon, the sun disappeared. Christine' *and Emma's* good friend, Nellie Edstrom, rushed over to tell the Floods that a forest fire had burned Hinckley and was on its way to Sandstone. That was the last time Christine *and Emma* would see their dear friend.

"Strong winds roared around them as the Flood family ran for the shelter of their root cellar. The family discussed the possibility that the Hinckley Fire had spawned a tornado. After several minutes in the root cellar, it became very hot and they began pouring the milk stored in the cellar over themselves to cool off. The heat grew steadily more intense.

"The Floods soon realized they must escape the cellar or die. John pushed on the trap door and found the door was stuck. He worked furiously to open the door. Just about the time he was almost giving up, the trap door finally burst open. Their house and the white picket fence surrounding the house were in flames.

"John and Eva Flood grabbed Christine's sister *Alvina* (three), and ran for the river. Christine's brothers, John Jr. (seventeen) and Oscar (nineteen), grabbed Christine (eleven) *and Emma* (thirteen) and followed their parents. Christine's parents reached the safety of the river with little *Alvina*, but to their horror could not find Christine, young John, Oscar, *or Emma*. It took several people to hold Eva Flood down to keep her from running back into the flames to save her children.

"As young John and Oscar ran down the river road, Oscar ran ahead. Sandy Gunn came along and took one of Christine's hands and John Jr. held the other. Afterward, Christine said that her feet never touched the ground all the way to the river. Eva and John cried with relief when their children jumped into the river to safety.

"Suddenly someone screamed, 'The dynamite shed, oh God, the dynamite.' Several men leaped up from the water to the nearby quarry shed and threw the boxes of explosives into the river.

Bridge over the Kettle River before trees had been cut. | Hinckley Fire Museum

"Minutes later, Christine heard and then saw a train approach the burning bridge over the Kettle. The survivors looked on in horror as the train crossed the flame-enveloped bridge. Seconds after the train crossed, the wooden bridge collapsed into the river.

"The Sandstone survivors spent a cold damp night in the Kettle River."[12]

Heros, Survivors, and Unexpected Aid

There were many heroes that day. Tommy Dunn, the telegraph operator stationed in the St. Paul and Duluth Depot in Hinckley, tried to save as many lives as possible. Out of loyalty, he stayed at his post too long and perished. Ed Barry and Bill Best, engineers on the Eastern Minnesota Train (a division of the Great Northern), and James Root, an engineer on the St. Paul and Duluth Road Railroad (later the Northern Pacific) were instrumental heroes, too. Root saved his passengers by piloting his burning train backwards five miles through fire and smoke from Hinckley to the safety of Skunk Lake. Barry and Best heroically drove a train, which was the combination of two engines, over the Kettle River High bridge in Sandstone. Barry's engine pulled from the front and Best's pushed from the back as the train crossed over the bridge. With the bridge on fire, they only had seconds to traverse the 850-foot span across the gorge, which was 132 feet above water and rocks. The five hundred people on board the train were only saved by these engineers' enormous courage.

My grandmother often told my cousin and me how the family ran for refuge in the Kettle River, even though it was low from drought. While in the water, Emma watched the fire jump across the river and create a burning canopy of trees. Emma said that whenever she looked up into the sky, all she could see were flames. During the worst moments, she would submerge. However, whenever she would lift her head out of the water for air, her hair would catch on fire and soot and smoke would fill her mouth. She said that the heavy smoke made it nearly impossible to breathe. All she could do was cough and choke.

Other reports amplified Emma's account, stating, "For a [full] hour the flames remained, as if hanging in the air above us, rolling back and forth across the river. We had to remain in the river for a [full] four hours and several times, because of the boundless heat, we [had to] submerge our heads under the water for as long as we were able to hold our breath."[20]

Larsen went on to write, "As the sun rose over the valley, they [the Flood family] began to make their way to the town of Banning. When they arrived in Banning, the residents did the best they could to make breakfast for the exhausted refugees. Christine said the Banning hotel served the refugees baking powder biscuits, and they were delightful.

"The survivors from Sandstone left the hotel and then walked to Groningen to meet the relief train to Duluth. Almost everyone boarded the train. As the train pulled out, the Flood family's dog, who had survived the fire with the family, ran alongside the train as long as he was able.

"When Christine got to Duluth, a home had been found for her separate from her family. She said she cried most of the time even though the family who had taken her in was very nice to her.

"Christine's father (John Flood) returned to Sandstone after a few days and found the family dog waiting for him at the site where the Flood family home had stood. (Eva and the children stayed in Duluth all winter and returned to Sandstone in the spring.)

"The Floods had lost everything but their lives. The grand house on the hill with its white picket fence, as well as John's saloon and meat market, were all gone. Also destroyed were Christine's lovely school clothes.

"After she returned to Sandstone, Christine learned that her best friend, Nellie Edstrom, had died in the fire with her family. The Edstroms had taken shelter in their well. When Mr. Edstrom climbed out of the well to take a look, he must have realized the danger to his family. He was found dead several feet from the well with his hands and forearms burned off as he had crawled through the flames to get his family out of the well.

"The Floods rebuilt their house on the same hilltop site where it stood until the 1970s when the Sandstone Volunteer Fire Department burned the old house during a drill."[12]

From the Ashes…

I can't imagine how my grandparents or other Pine County residents even began to assimilate the tragedy of the Hinckley fire. Although grateful for their lives, these simple folks must have been overwhelmed by the loss of their homes, loved ones, neighbors, and businesses. I know that after seven years of extremely hard work, my own family was proud of the new life they had built.

September 1, 1894, had been a day of shattered dreams. It is unbelievable that everything these pioneers owned or built was wiped out in one afternoon. The question today is, "How did they and so many others find the will or capacity to begin again?"

Perhaps the answer to that question begins with "character." Although these simple farmers and men of the forests may have been uneducated and unrefined, they were extremely courageous, capable, and tough. They were a wise people who had an intrinsic bond with the land—whether it be prairie or forest. They were just the right type of people America needed as it expanded farther and farther to the north and west.

During the fire's aftermath, fire relief houses were built and donated to the destitute people of Sandstone. These houses came in two sizes. The Floods were granted one of the larger ones. This new home was built on the Floods' original home site on First Street and continued to be operated as a boarding house. I don't know what happened to the saloon, but it is recorded that a "Flod and Anderson's Meat Market" was added to the second story of the Opera house a year after the fire in 1895.

Lessons Learned: Conservation Begins

Near the end of the 1800s, disasters like these made people in Minnesota realize that forests and prairies have a complex ecological relationship. Natural resources depend upon that relationship. Denuded landscapes were seen to have brought on drought, insect infestation, wildlife extinction, poor soil, and tragic fires.

Conservation began in the United States when the first national park was formed by President Ulysses S. Grant. On March 1, 1872, he signed the Yellowstone National Park Protection Act into law. Although it took many more years, in 1911 the Minnesota Forest Service (MFS), a forerunner of the Department of Natural Resources, was formed. "With a small but dedicated force of foresters and forest firefighters, they enforced new and stricter laws governing slash removal; regulated railroads to prevent sparks from locomotives, requiring burning permits, and created Forest Ranger Districts throughout the north woods."[14] In 1931, the Minnesota Department of Conservation was founded. Shortly thereafter, leaders from fields such as forestry, agronomy, geology, and hydrology brought their expertise to federal resource policy.

6

Marriage

EMMA FLOOD and CHARLES SODERBERG WED

As fate would have it, two years after the fire, my teenage grandmother, Emma Flood, helped serve dinner to one of the new lodgers in her family's rebuilt boarding house. This young man was a Swedish immigrant named Charles (Charlie) Soderberg. Charlie had left Sweden in 1892 and recently arrived in Sandstone (1896) where he was hired to work in the sandstone quarry.

Physically, Charlie was not a tall man, but had a very muscular and sturdy build. True to the Swedish stereotype, he had white-blonde hair and light blue eyes. On the other hand, Emma was a tall woman with a round face and brown hair. I once read that people from western Dahlsland were known for their distinctive features. They had an inclination toward brown eyes, dark hair, and a slightly rounder face.

I don't know where my grandfather lived or worked during the four-year span between Sweden and Sandstone; but I do know that he was thrilled to find a job within Sandstone's growing community. He also considered it his good fortune to meet a lovely Swedish girl named Emma Flood. Although there was a ten-year difference in age, Charlie and Emma eventually fell in love. They were married three years later in Duluth on July 8,1899. Emma was eighteen, and Charlie turned twenty-eight the day following their simple wedding.

The Sandstone Quarry

As mentioned previously, William H. Grant opened the Kettle River quarries in Sandstone during the summer of 1885. However, it only took one year for him to realize the costliness of the operation. In 1886, Grant went into partnership with John P. Knowles of St. Paul.

But even under the new partnership, within only a few years, Grant and Knowles saw that more capital was needed. They first entered into a ten-year leasing arrangement for a five-hundred-foot frontage on the banks of the Kettle River with a Minneapolis Contracting firm—Ring and Tobin. Shortly thereafter, they went into a partnership with two Pine City men and incorporated to form the Kettle River Sandstone Company. At that time, Grant reported, "… orders for building stone are coming in at a lively rate." (Sixteen railroad cars were loaded with sandstone every day.)[12]

Apparently, financial problems continued to loom. In 1888, the Kettle River Sandstone Company agreed to lease the quarry operation to Ring and Tobin. At that point, Grant resigned as director and president. Ring and Tobin operated the quarry with good success until the financial panic of 1893, when their bank failed and the company's creditors forced the quarry to shut down. Thankfully, the very next year, another group of investors saw the quarry's tremendous potential and reorganized it as the Minnesota Sandstone Company.

Working for the Minnesota Sandstone Company

Charlie Soderberg began to work in the quarry two years after the quarry was renamed the Minnesota Sandstone Company. It was an exciting time for Charlie and for the town of Sandstone. The new owners had started an aggressive marketing campaign that earned the local sandstone a reputation as being one of the best building stones available. Orders began to pour in. The town of Sandstone may have only had three hundred residents when the Floods arrived in 1888, but by 1895, the population had increased to 1,058.

For a jobless immigrant who spoke very little English, the quarry was a wonderful means for steady employment. The first summer Charlie worked in the quarry, a full crew of quarrymen and thirty-five stone cutters began a contract for a library at the University of Illinois in Urbana, Illinois.

As a point of interest—sixty-five years later, I was a student at the U of I. At that time, I did not realize that the beautiful old building named Altgeld Hall had a connection to my grandfather and the sandstone quarry.

In 1958, the building was no longer a library, but was used for science and mathematics.

About the time Charlie started to work in the quarry, a laborer's pay was $1.35 a day, while the more highly skilled drillers earned $1.50 a day. Since the quarry was usually closed in the winter, many of the quarry workers were transients. Some workers commuted back to their homes in Great Britain, Germany, Sweden, and other European countries.

As the quarry company grew, it employed up to three hundred men. It met contracts for huge orders such as coping stone for railroad and wagon bridges. By the end of the summer of 1898, the quarry was not only shipping large stone for buildings, but also three hundred thousand paving blocks and four hundred cars of crushed rock a day.

With this success, the company began to remain open the entire winter. It increased wages and began to offer better working conditions. Now a first-class stone-cutter was paid $3 per day, and his work days were reduced from ten to nine hours. The noon lunch break was increased from thirty to forty-five minutes.

Early Family Life

A year after Emma and Charlie's marriage, a 1900 census record shows that the young married couple, along with a "baby Soderberg," were living with Eva and John Flood and their two daughters, Christina and Alvina. The Floods must have still been operating a boarding house, as seven men were also listed as living in the same household.

After their marriage, Charlie worked six days a week in the quarry. He proved himself to be a steady worker and a good provider, and in 1901 he purchased a home. The next census record shows that the Soderberg family now included three children (two daughters and a son). I was told that as the children grew, they would walk to the quarry each day with their father's lunch.

Work in the sandstone quarry may have offered a steady income, but it was fraught with dangerous, unhealthy conditions. There were fatalities due to equipment accidents, injuries suffered from falling rocks, and burns from kerosene or black powder explosions. Stonecutters often died from silicosis, a chronic lung disease caused by prolonged inhalation of silica dust. Thankfully, Grandpa Charlie worked in the quarry for many years without harm.

Middle figure, Charlie Soderberg, 1907.

Charlie's Passion for the Wilderness

Although Charlie only worked as a laborer in Sandstone, he was well-skilled in carpentry and farming. And, ever since he was a child in Sweden, his true passion was the outdoors. It was not a coincidence that Charlie was drawn to the lakes and forests of northern Minnesota. He loved everything about the wilderness. No matter how busy Charlie was working or caring for his family, he always found time to fish, hunt, explore, and trap.

The Soderberg dinner table was never empty. Charlie provided his family with an abundance of fish, duck, grouse, venison, and other wildlife. In fact, a 1907 Pine County newspaper photo highlighted Charlie and his friends after a successful hunting trip. They are pictured standing proudly with a bounty of bear and deer.

The Soderberg Home

I remember my grandparents' home in Sandstone. It was a two-story white wooden structure with a large screened-in front porch. The house was located at 306 First Street on a large corner lot, only a few blocks away from the Flood family home. (Ironically, the house was destroyed by an arsonist in 2003.) As a young mother, it must have been convenient for Emma Soderberg to live only a short distance from her parents and younger sister Alvina. No matter how busy Emma was during her day, there was always time for a cup of coffee with family and friends. After her marriage, Christine, or "Sissy," (Emma's younger sister), and her family also lived nearby. The extended family was always very close and supportive of each other.

All of Emma and Charlie's children were born at home. By 1910, the Soderberg's family now numbered four children: Violet (eleven), Floyd (ten), Helen

1908: Violet, Helen, Floyd and Carl.

(six), and Carl (four). My mother, Eva Soderberg, was born a year later in 1911. She was the last child.

As wonderful as it was for Emma to have her own home, in the beginning she did not have any modern conveniences. There was no hot running water or an indoor bathroom. In fact, the family was without electricity, and used only kerosene lamps. In the evening, in order to preserve kerosene, everyone sat together in one room with one lamp. Of course, in the winter, it was too cold to use the outhouse, so a chamber pot was kept under each bed.

Laundry too was a complicated issue. Without hot water, Emma would have to first heat water on the stove and then pour it into a large metal tub that sat on a wooden table in the kitchen. My first memory of Sandstone is of my grandmother and mother bathing me as a toddler in this tub. After adding the sheets and clothes to the tub, Grandma would take a long wooden stick and mix the laundry back and forth, over and over. For especially tough stains, she had to use a metal washboard. With five children and a husband who worked in a quarry, it usually took Emma all day to wash clothes. Emma probably worked just as many long hours as Charlie—if not more.

When the Soderberg children were young, they were taught to believe in Santa Claus. My grandmother would have them write letters to Santa

1901: Emma and Charlie's home at 309 First St., Sandstone.

and then burn them in the stove. She assured the children that the smoke went directly to Santa's house, and he could read each message.

Christmas gifts were pretty simple. One year, my mother's sister, Helen, only received an orange. Yet, Christmas was a special time for the family. Each year, the Christmas tree was lit with real candles. One year, my mother, Eva, was chosen to play Santa Lucia. She wore a crown of candles in her hair, which symbolically prepared the way for Christmastide.

The 1940s

Surprisingly, even by the 1940s, Emma still cooked on a woodstove. Along with preparing large hearty dinners, Emma always found time to bake mouthwatering cakes, pies, cookies, biscuits, and sweet rolls. As a Chicago child, I was amazed that she was able to create such wonders using a primitive oven without any temperature controls. Emma rose very early every morning to light her fires. She knew the secret for keeping wood at just the right temperature, and she became known for baking the lightest biscuits and the tallest lemon meringue pies.

In the 1940s, Emma still used blocks of ice for refrigeration. My older cousin Andrene noted, "The iceman would come around a couple of times a week in the summer. Grandma would put a card in her window to tell him how many pounds of ice she wanted. Either five, ten, fifteen, or twenty-five pounds of ice. The iceman had a horse and cart filled with blocks of ice. He put a large piece of leather on his shoulder and back, and then, using giant tongs he would load the ice on his shoulder and put the large block of ice in Grandma's icebox (a lidded box which was located in a small breezeway off the kitchen). In the summer, all the kids would follow the iceman because he would give them slivers of ice."

Andrene told me that it was many years before Emma and Charlie finally had a bathroom installed in their home. In the early 1940s, they converted a third bedroom into a beautiful bathroom. Emma was so excited that she would go up and down the stairs just to admire this modern convenience. She also made it a point to clean the sink, toilet, and bathtub over and over, every day, until they shined.

Whenever I visited Sandstone, I rarely saw Emma without an apron. Not only did Emma provide her family three meals a day, but she maintained a garden and spent hours canning vegetables and fruit, which were stored in the family root cellar. This cellar was accessed through a trapdoor in the dining room floor.

As a child, I was always intrigued by this cellar, which I considered a hidden, secret room. There was a set of steep stairs that led down to a small basement-type room with a dirt floor. I have to admit, as I descended the stairs, it sometimes felt a bit creepy— especially if my head hit a network of cobwebs. One day, Andrene saw a snake crawling on the floor. She refused to ever go down again. This dark, dank room with its constant coolness may have seemed ominous, but it provided the perfect place to store potatoes, root vegctables, and Grandma's canned goods.

Teaching Wilderness Skills

My grandfather loved his daughters, but he adored his sons. They adored him too. The boys were six years apart in age, and when they both were quite young, Charlie began to teach them the same outdoor skills he had learned as a boy in Sweden. Children were not coddled in those days, and it wasn't long before Floyd and Carl spent as much time as possible hunting and fishing on their own. They, too, grew to feel at one with the lakes and forests of Minnesota, and proved themselves to be fearless. In fact, one day Carl decided to show his prowess by jumping off a bridge into the Kettle River. Regrettably, he seriously broke his leg and had a metal plate for the rest of his life.

All of the Soderberg children were taught to embrace the outdoors. Once they finished their schoolwork and chores, they were given free reign. Perhaps, between the three Soderberg girls, my mother, Eva, was more

Gretchen Berg and Eva Soderberg.

Carl, using a cane, with Charlie and Emma.

like her brothers. While the boys spent all their time exploring the woods or fishing on the lakes and rivers, Eva's favorite things were ice skating, picking blueberries, roasting a baked potato on stick over an open fire, and swimming in the Kettle River or Grindstone Lake.

As a child, Eva hitched her German shepherd dog, Jack, to a sled and trained him to pull her through the snow. She also had a pair of black racing skates with long blades. She and her best friend and cousin, Gretchen Berg, loved to pretend they could skate as fast as the wind. (In later years, as much as my mother loved to ice skate, she refused to switch over to modern figure skates. She held onto her black racing skates for the rest of her life.)

7

Changing Times and Economic Hardship

Emma's father, John Flood, died in 1905 at the age of fifty-four. His wife Eva was left to care for their two daughters, Christine (twenty-one) and Alvina (thirteen). Although I do not know the cause of John's death, I note that typhoid fever, diphtheria, and cholera were reported to be present in Sandstone in 1906.

By the time of John's death, the Flood boys had already left Sandstone. Young John and Oscar had both moved to Minneapolis, where John went into the upholstery business. Eventually, he founded a company called Northwestern Upholstery Co., which became very successful. Christine (Sissy) Flood married Guttorm Berg in 1909 and continued to live in Sandstone. In later years, she lived with and cared for her mother, Eva.

When Emma Flood married Charlie Soderberg, Sandstone was quickly becoming a boomtown. As Sandstone continued to grow and prosper, the Soderberg family grew and prospered right along with it. Charlie was even able to purchase a small piece of farmland east of town.

The Quarry Closes

On January 1, 1903, the Minnesota Sandstone Company reorganized and became the Kettle River Quarries Company. Afterwards, the new company saw the need to diversify. Up until that time, millions of square yards of sandstone paving blocks had been shipped from the quarry for paving the streets of major cities in several states, as well as those in Minneapolis, St. Paul, and Duluth. Demands changed, however, and there became an increasing market for wooden streets and sidewalks. In order to keep up with the times, a creosote plant was built to produce tamarack wood paving blocks, as well as poles and railway ties.

The new company became successful and doubled their business by opening another creosote plant in Madison, Illinois. By January 1910, during the busiest, most profitable year of the local quarries and creosote plant, the Kettle River Quarries Company once again changed their name. Now they were to be known as the Kettle River Company.

Unfortunately, this was the start of the quarry's decline. In 1911 (the year my mother, Eva Soderberg, was born), concrete and structural steel were found to be more economical. Once again, this drastically reduced the demand for massive building stone. "The high costs of explosives, keeping the drills and saws sharp, and rising railroad rates made it impossible to stay competitive. A decrease in orders for the creosote plant, a stone-cutters strike in 1914, and World War I also contributed to the company's problems."[12]

In 1919, all quarry operations stopped. During the 1920s and 1930s, the quarry tried to continue to operate. The company saw it could fill the demand for coarse Kettle River crushed rock, and would benefit from adding a concrete manufacturing plant. But, during that period, little building stone was shipped. (The last stone was removed from the quarry in 1976.)

After 1919, the town of Sandstone and men like Charlie began to suffer from the loss of what had been a major source of employment and revenue.

For Emma, this meant that "survival" once again became a theme in her life. Emma had faced the famines of Sweden, a deadly disease while crossing the Atlantic, a raging fire in Minnesota, and now the loss of income due to a capricious demand for rock.

World War I

In 1914, as work in the quarry continued to wane, an international conflict broke out in Europe. The Central Powers, mainly led by Germany, Austria–Hungary, and Turkey, fought against Allied countries such as Great Britain, Russia, France, and Italy. In the early years of this war, President Woodrow Wilson declared that the United States would remain neu-

Floyd Soderberg, 1917.

Alvina Flod, 1913.

tral. Yet many Americans contributed to relief efforts. Some volunteered as ambulance drivers, nurses, or even as pilots and soldiers.

Around 1913, Emma's youngest sister, Alvina Flood, married a young Sandstone man named Butch Stenmark. Alvina was a vivacious, beautiful woman who was a great joy to her family. For some reason, while America remained neutral, Butch joined the fighting in Europe and was killed in Belgium around 1914.

Alvina and Butch had been deeply in love. After learning about Butch's death, Alvina became inconsolable. That same year, she was diagnosed with tuberculosis and died at the early age of twenty-three.

Around the start of World War I, my mother's two older sisters, Violet (eighteen) and Helen (thirteen), left Sandstone. Violet went to Minneapolis, married, and shortly thereafter settled near San Francisco where she and her husband, as an avocation, had a gold mine.

Helen also moved to Minneapolis and eventually worked in a department store called Young and Quinlan. Department stores were a huge part of Minnesota history. The 1920s were known to be the Golden Age of home-grown Minnesota department stores. They included Donaldson's, Powers, Schuneman's, Young and Quinlan, and Dayton's.

Steamer Juniata, *Duluth Superior Harbor.* | from postcard

Teenager Floyd Soderberg Joins the Navy

On April 6, 1917, the United States declared war on Germany and entered World War I. America sent more than a million troops to Europe. Whether out of a sense of duty to his country, or as a way to ease the financial burden on his parents, in May 1917, the Soderberg's eldest son, Floyd, lied about his age and joined the Navy. He was only seventeen. That was the same month Congress passed the Selective Service Act, registering men between the ages of twenty-one to thirty for service in World War I. Knowing that my uncle Floyd was an extremely generous and loving son, I was not surprised to learn that even at the early age of seventeen, Floyd began sending money home.

Floyd loved the Navy. He loved ships, being at sea, and having a good camaraderie with his shipmates. During the war, the US Navy conveyed troops and supplies to France and Italy, and focused on countering enemy U-boats in the Atlantic Ocean and the Mediterranean Sea. Floyd served on several ships during the war and spent some time in France. These ships included the *USS Nebraska*, the *USS Iowan*, and the *USS Graf Walsersee.*

Floyd was formally discharged from the Navy in November 1919, the same year the sandstone quarry closed. In what should have been a happy and carefree time, he, along with other returning military, faced a two-year-post-World War I recession (1920–21). In short, there were few jobs

Charles Soderberg farming and hunting in Cook County.

available as the economy could not absorb the millions of returning veterans. At some point in the early 1920s, Floyd began to work on the ships that plied the Great Lakes. With his Naval experience and love of being at sea, this was a perfect fit.

Great Lakes Shipping

Great Lakes shipping has come a long way since French missionaries and fur traders explored the uncharted waters of the five Great Lakes in their canoes and small boats.

Even the grand sloops and schooners of the British were eventually replaced by greater American vessels called steamers and lakers. Today, the largest vessels on the Great Lakes are the thousand footers. Depending on water levels, these massive ships can carry as much as 78,850 long tons of bulk cargo.

My uncle Floyd worked on Great Lake boats off and on during the 1920s. I was told that he eventually became a wheelsman. I still have a postcard he wrote to his mother, Emma, in 1928. The photo on the card is of the steamer Juniata, which sailed out of the Duluth-Superior Harbor. In this card, Floyd wrote that he had just shipped out on the *Elba*, with a good chance to go to Chicago.

Farming

While Floyd was starting to find work on the Great Lakes, my grandfather, Charlie, who was no longer working at the quarry, decided to start farming a small piece of land he owned just east of Sandstone. Previously, he had built a large shed-like structure on the property. Carl, his youngest son, was still living at home, along with my mother, Eva. Carl helped Charlie with the planting.

The 1920s were the beginning of some very financially lean years for the Soderberg family. By winter of the mid-1920s, neither Charlie, Floyd, nor Carl could find any work. It was then that Floyd and his younger brother Carl decided to head to the northern forests of Cook County. They felt confident that they had the necessary skills to hunt, trap, and survive a winter in the wilderness.

8

Into the Wilderness— Grand Marais & Durfee Creek

According to my mother, Floyd Soderberg first came to the Grand Marais area as a teenager while hunting with his father, Charlie. My older cousin Carlene—Carl Soderberg's daughter—believes that Floyd first saw Grand Marais while working on the Great Lakes ships. Perhaps in some way both stories are true. No matter what, when, or how, once Floyd experienced the wilderness area surrounding Grand Marais, the Gunflint Trail became his focus and passion for the rest of his life.

I recently found a November 1926 newspaper notice stating that Carl and Floyd Soderberg went to Cook County to trap. Later it was reported that they returned home in January due to the great amount of snow. The truth was, as previously mentioned, jobs were scarce and the young men felt they could survive winter in one of Minnesota's most remote forests. Floyd was twenty-six and Carl was twenty.

The Trapper's Cabin

It would appear that Floyd and Carl drove directly from Sandstone to Grand Marais, where they found a road to Durfee Creek. (Either a road just east of town off Highway 61, or a road off the Gunflint Trail where County Road 60 intersects today.) Somewhere near Durfee Creek, the brothers found an empty trapper's cabin and moved right in. Interestingly, in the

Carl and Floyd at home in the trapper's cabin.

Floyd brewing coffee outside.

The brothers sawing wood.

1980s, early Grand Marais resident Emerson Morris told me that this very same trapper's cabin could still be found in the woods.

I am fortunate to have several photos of Floyd and Carl while they lived in the trapper's cabin. One is of the two brothers standing by their Model T during a heavy snowstorm. Others show the interior and exterior of the trapper's cabin. There are photos of the young men chopping wood in the snow, cooking coffee on an open fire outside, and shooting game while on skis. Surprisingly, with all the cold weather and deep snow, the boys looked warm and content while they sat in front of a small woodstove in that rough-hewn cabin. I'm sure that besides trapping, Floyd and Carl spent a good deal of time hunting, ice fishing, and

Arriving at Durfee Creek for the winter—1926.

just plain exploring. If the newspaper notice was correct, sometime in January the brothers returned to Sandstone because of the deep snow.

A Vow to Return to the Gunflint Trail

At the end of their experience, both Floyd and Carl admitted they absolutely loved living in

Carl—hunting on skis.

the wilderness. In fact, that winter in the woods became a watershed—a defining time for them both. Before they left Grand Marais, these adventurous brothers made a vow to each other. Someday they would return and live permanently on the Gunflint Trail.

I love what poet Henry David Thoreau said about time spent in the woods: "I took a walk in the woods and came out taller than the trees." I believe the Soderberg family always felt a profound sense of solace and freedom whenever they spent time in the wilderness. They truly recognized that the technology and ease of a sophisticated civilization could never compare to the wonderment of living in a simple cabin in the woods.

Emma in Lincoln Park.

And yes, every time they walked out of those woods, they stood taller than the trees.

Economic Solutions: Chicago

Shortly after their winter experience at Durfee Creek, Floyd and Carl moved to Chicago where they were able to secure jobs. Carl found work as a carpenter and Floyd became an apprentice in the trade of laying carpet and tile. Both were happy to find well-paying jobs with steady work, and persuaded their father in Sandstone to come too.

Charlie took their advice and spent a few summers working in Chicago and living in the Lincoln Park area with his wife, Emma, and their teenage daughter, my mother, Eva. As an accomplished carpenter, Charlie was hired to work on several Chicago buildings, including Symphony Hall.

Of course, finding work in Chicago was only a means to an end for the Soderbergs. It allowed my grandparents, Charlie and Emma, to maintain their home in Sandstone, and offered Carl and Floyd a way to save money to someday return to the Gunflint Trail.

The Roaring Twenties

Perhaps no other city embodied the spirit of the 1920s in quite the same way as Chicago. The gangster Al Capone said it best. Chicago was "the city that put the roar in the Roaring Twenties." One could argue that Chicago defined the Jazz Age, Prohibition, and the mob. While living in Chicago, Emma shed her apron for a flapper dress. Eva learned to dance the Charleston, and Carl made bathtub gin. During that time, Floyd and Carl became popular with the ladies. They took their dates to speakeasies and to the beaches of Lake Michigan to swim. However, every block of vacation was spent returning to the Gunflint Trail.

Emma, Eva and Charlie in Chicago.

The Great Depression

Unfortunately, in September 1929 the "roar" in Chicago stopped. The stock market crashed and triggered the start of the Great Depression, which continued for nearly ten years. This was a devastating time for families everywhere on all economic levels. Yet, it seems that no matter how tough things became, all of the Soderbergs continued to find employment.

The Tornado

Although Charlie worked in Chicago in the winters, he returned to Sandstone during the warmer months and tended to his farmland. Unfortunately, in 1930, tragedy struck. One day while Charlie was out in the fields, he realized that a serious storm was coming quickly. He ran to his farm shed to take refuge. After only a short while, he heard what sounded like a loud train. Puzzled, he opened the door to see what was causing the sound. As he did, a tornado blasted apart the shed and sent him sailing across the sky. According to my mother, he awoke about a mile away (probably more like the length of a football field). By some miracle he survived, but he suffered broken ribs and a head injury. A few years later, he began to experience a series of strokes that left him using a cane and having difficulty speaking.

George Cleaver and Eva Soderberg.

Love and Marriage

The Great Depression did not stop the Soderberg children from pursuing love and marriage. Floyd began a serious relationship with a divorced woman named Helen Doody. Although the romance did not last, throughout his life he remained a loving surrogate father to her two sons, Herb and Gene Doody. (Gene would later become a popular figure in Grand Marais and the Gunflint Trail.)

In 1931, Carl fell in love and married a Chicago girl—Eleanor Pusner. Three years later, their only child, Carlene, was born.

After graduating from Sandstone High School in 1930, my mother, Eva, began to work in Chicago too. For several years, Eva did secretarial work for a railroad and took advantage of free passes to visit her sister Violet in San Francisco. Eva was a very attractive woman who had extraordinary ice-blue eyes, blonde hair, and was naturally slim. One of her dates during that time was with the famous football legend Red Grange, known as the "Galloping Ghost."

In 1932, Eva began dating a man named George Cleaver. George was a bond trader with a brokerage firm in Chicago. He came from a well-educated family with a background completely opposite of Eva's. While they were dating, my parents enjoyed the Chicago nightlife. One evening, they visited a small nightclub where they watched the performance of a new comedian named Red Skelton. After the show, Red stopped by their table to say hello and ended up joining them for dinner.

Eva and George also loved to go to the movies. On July 22, 1934, my parents made plans to attend the Biograph Theater to see the movie Manhattan Melodrama, a "gang and gun" film, starring Clark Gable, William Powell, and Myrna Loy. However, just before they left for the evening, my parents had a lover's quarrel and George ended up going to the movie by himself.

When my father arrived at the theater, he saw several suspicious-looking men loitering nearby and he warned the person selling tickets to beware. The agent scoffed and merely waved him off. This was the same night the notorious gangster John Dillinger and the "lady in red" chose to attend the Biograph Theater. The men my father saw were FBI agents who had set up a sting. When Dillinger exited the theater that night, the agents moved in to arrest him. Dillinger attempted to flee, drew a gun, and was killed.

Three months later, in October of 1934, Eva and George Cleaver eloped. Unbelievably, they kept their marriage a secret for five years. It seems Eva would have lost her job with the railroad if it was known that she was married. I was not born until 1940.

Elinor, Floyd, Carlene, and Carl.

Floyd, Charlie, and Carl.

9

Early Camping on the Gunflint Trail

During the summers in the 1930s, the Soderbergs, along with their girl-friends, spouses, and children, could all be found camping on the Gunflint Trail. I have many family photos of the Soderbergs at campgrounds such as West Bearskin or Flour Lake. In those photos, great stringers of fish were proudly displayed while the women, including my mother, wore dresses and sometimes sturdy shoes with a high heel.

I don't know how any of these ladies ever managed to portage, fish, or canoe in a dress. In later photos, my mother was seen in more practical clothes such as knickers and boots. Referring to the 1930s, my family

Helen, Gene, and Herb Doody.

often spoke of knowing some of the early Gunflint Trail resort owners in-cluding Charlie Boostrom of Clearwater Lodge, Jesse Gapin of Hungry Jack Lodge, Doc Rempel of Old Northwoods Lodge, and the Stapletons of Loon Lake Lodge.

CCC Camps

Today, anyone who loves camping on the Gunflint Trail and exploring the Superior National Forest should give thanks to President Franklin D. Roosevelt. Ninety years ago, on April 5, 1933, Roosevelt signed a bill for the establishment of the Civilian Conservation Corps (CCC), which was devised to relieve poverty and unemployment among young men during the height of the Great Depression. "The CCC program left a lasting effect as a result of its work. Along the Gunflint Trail the CCC left many recreational camp sites and a vast network of easily traveled portages that continue to be enjoyed by countless tourists. Their work provided an infrastructure that enabled the creation of the Boundary Waters Canoe Area Wilderness to provide both natural conservation of the Superior National Forest and a means for outdoor minded people to enjoy its benefits."[24]

To qualify for the CCC program, candidates had to meet certain standards. The men had to be between the ages of eighteen and twenty-five, a US citizen, out of school, unemployed, not married, and on public assistance. Once selected, recruits reported to an assigned camp for a period of six months. Those with a good work record had the option to sign up for a second six-month term. Each man received thirty dollars per month but was required to send twenty-five dollars home to their families. The remaining five dollars was for their own personal use.

The Minnesota CCC program peaked in 1935 with 104 active camps. The first Cook County CCC camp was located at Caribou Lake, near Lutsen, in May, 1933. Shortly after, six camps were established along or near the Gunflint Trail. The first three Gunflint Trail camps began in June—Northern Light, Gunflint, and Cascade. A month later, Poplar Lake Camp was built on the west end of Poplar Lake. It did not consist of CCC boys but of Army veterans from the Spanish–American War and World War I. By the fall of 1935, two other Gunflint Trail camps were built—one at Cross River with men from Missouri and Arkansas, and the other near Seagull Lake.

For the most part, each camp barrack could house two hundred men, and a camp could grow to include fifteen buildings. Normally, in addition to four or five barracks, there would be a kitchen, mess hall, officer quarters, dispensary, recreational hall, school building, lavatory, bathhouse, and latrine. There was also a camp canteen that sold personal items.

A typical work day was eight hours long. The day began at 6:00 a.m. with exercise and breakfast. Morning and afternoon work sessions were followed by breaks for lunch and supper. Noon meals would be served at worksites if these were located a good distance from camp. The young men were offered free time for recreation and study in the evening, but lights out was at 9:30 p.m.

Although Minnesota CCC projects centered mainly on forestry and state and national park projects, they also supported soil and water conservation. Men in forest camps cut and cleared brush to help conserve existing forests, and planted 124 million trees. They participated in tree disease prevention programs, built roads and portage trails, and fought forest fires. In fact, 123 thousand man-days were invested in forest fire fighting. Fire prevention efforts included clearing deadwood and building water towers, ranger stations, and firebreaks.

Those of us who have hiked or portaged in the Superior National Forest should be grateful to the men who created this wonderful network of trail systems, which we so often take for granted today. The July 1938 issue of the Gunflint Camp newspaper contained an article about constructing one such trail.

"It's 7:45 in the morning and all the fellows are waiting for the work whistle to blow, WHEE-EE-EE, there it goes. We hop into our trucks and are off to a day on the trail.

"We reach our destination and are assigned to our jobs. The foreman assigns two or three men to take brush hooks, axes, and a cross cut saw to go ahead to clear the right away [sic] for the rest of the crew. These fellows cut down all brush and trees within three feet on each side of the stakes [designated the center of the trail placed by crew foreman] leaving a path six feet wide. The rest of the boys each take a mattock [like a pickax] and start leveling off where the brush has been cleared. The path is to be 16 inches wide, using the marking stakes for a guiding line.

"The trail has to be made as level as possible so when a man is portaging a canoe or anything else he can walk with ease and without fear of falling or stumbling over rocks or roots. After the trail has been grubbed and leveled out, one or two men go back with wheelbarrows, shovel and dig sand from the most convenient place so they can fill in where rocks and rotten logs have been lying in the trail. There also is a man with a rock hammer, he goes ahead and breaks all rocks sticking out of the ground, and that are too heavy to move. This procedure continues until the trail is completely finished."[24]

Carl Soderberg.

George and Eva Soderberg Cleaver.

Eva Soderberg Joins Her Brothers Camping

After my mother's first trip up the Gunflint Trail, like her brothers, she found that she, too, had a deep connection to the wilderness. Although Eva loved fishing, camping, and canoeing, she could be happy just sitting alone in the midst of the deep woods. Throughout her life, Eva remained in awe of the giant pines that filled the forests, the trails that led to remote, hidden lakes, the skies that turned into a blanket of stars at night, and the unexpected appearance of wildlife. Mosquitoes never bothered her, and she often commented that nothing tasted better than a meal cooked over an open campfire.

As a newlywed, my father, George Cleaver, had no choice but to embrace the wilderness. Luckily, he had two great mentors—my uncles Floyd and Carl. It wasn't long before George could keep up with Eva. In fact, within a few years, George invited his own family to join in on the camping fun. One of the icons of the Jazz Age was the ukulele, and George learned how to play the instrument. The Cleavers all had beautiful voices and would happily join George every evening for a songfest around the campfire.

Charlie and Eva enroute to the Gunflint Trail.

One of my mother's favorite stories regarding those early camping experiences was the time she and my father, along with a party that included her brothers, Carl and Floyd, were stranded by a terrible storm deep in the Boundary Waters. Her father, Charles, was to pick them up at a designated point on a particular afternoon. Even with the storm, Charlie arrived right on time and waited and waited for most of the day. By late evening, he was panic-stricken and feared the worst. Finally, around midnight, he caught sight of a group of canoeists challenging the whitecaps and rain. When they safely came to shore, he didn't know whether to hug them or berate them.

Eva and Charlie Soderberg.

My First Camping Trip: 1940

World wars, economic depressions, marriages, children—nothing could stop the Soderbergs from returning each summer to camp on the Gunflint Trail. In June 1940, my parents joined my grandfather and uncles, Carl and Floyd, for another trip. This time, my mother was expecting a baby—me—but was not aware that she was already about seven-and-a-half months along. Through a miscalculation, her doctor had concluded that I

Bears come for lunch.

would be born in October. To everyone's surprise, I was born full term in August. I doubt if it really would have mattered to my mother, as returning to Minnesota and camping each summer was a priority.

On that trip, one afternoon my mother decided to bake a cake and stayed alone at the campsite while the men went fishing. Just as she was frosting the cake, an aggressive bear came out of the woods looking for a sample. Eva decided it would be a good thing to hide in the woods while the bear finished off the cake.

I was born about eight weeks later with a great deal of black hair, which was a surprise to my blonde mother. In Eva's Swedish superstitious way, she decided that all my dark hair was caused by her fright of the bear.

10

World War II— 1939 to 1945

It is hard to believe that just as the Great Depression ended, World War II began. Looking back now, I understand why my parents' generation is referred to as the "greatest generation." These Americans lived through two world wars, an epidemic, and a severe economic depression. Ever since the American Revolution, no other generation has withstood such hardship, and they did so with uncomplaining resiliency and bravery.

Floyd Joins the Navy Again

World War II began on September 1, 1939, when Nazi Germany, under Adolf Hitler, invaded Poland. It continued for six years until Japan surrendered on September 2, 1945. Once again, Floyd Soderberg enlisted in the Navy and his grown surrogate sons, Gene and Herb Doody, enlisted with him. My father, George Cleaver, was too old for the draft, and Carl Soderberg was classified as 4F (deemed unfit to serve) because of a plate in his leg. I understand that Floyd, Herb, and Gene thought they would all be shipped out together. Unfortunately, this was not to be. Immediately, they were sent their separate ways.

I am not sure where Gene and Herb spent their time during the war, but sadly, Herb was killed. Floyd took part in Operation Torch, the Allied invasion of French North Africa. The goal of Operation Torch was to open a second front in Europe.

Gene and Herb Doody.

Floyd must have made a plan with my parents to let them know where he was going by using a secret code. Although I was only three years old, I have a clear memory of my parents receiving a letter from Floyd just before he shipped out. I remember my dad holding me in his arms as my mother held Floyd's letter up to a hot ceiling light. Excitedly, she exclaimed, "Africa. Floyd is on his way to Africa." It seems Floyd wrote the word "Africa" in milk on his letter. Milk on paper when exposed to strong light turns brown and can be read. (Not the safest tactic to use when a major secret military invasion is about to begin.)

Floyd was a Coxswain first class—a steersman on the USS Elizabeth Stanton, which landed her troops and equipment in Casablanca on November 8, 1942. After the successful invasion, Floyd spent several weeks in Casablanca. I still have his photo album that chronicles this time. It includes photos of burning ships, fellow sailors, a French general, local children, snake charmers, monkeys, and even a beautiful Arabian woman. While in North Africa, Floyd sent me a pair of Arabian slippers. The slippers were made of leather and had toes that curled upward. As a three-year-old, I loved them and felt like Aladdin whenever I put them on.

The War Years

Although the whole family was proud of Floyd for enlisting in the Second World War, they were terribly concerned about his safety. Back in Sandstone, every evening my grandfather would sit in front of a large radio in the living room and tune in to Gabriel Heatter's broadcast of the latest news. Charlie would lean close to the radio and listen intently to every word about the war. Everyone knew to be totally silent during this time as Charlie would hush anyone who tried to speak.

On May 8, 1945, I was sent to my grandparents' bedroom in Sandstone to take a nap. While asleep, I was awakened by car horns, sirens, and people yelling. I ran to the window and learned that this was V-E Day (victory in Europe Day). At last, the war had ended. It seems a makeshift parade of fire trucks, cars, and people decided to march down First Street in a spontaneous celebration. I have never forgotten that moment, because as I leaned out the window to get a better look, the window slipped and fell on my head. It took my mother a while to extricate me and then to dry my tears. Of course, in the end, I too was elated—my uncle Floyd was coming home.

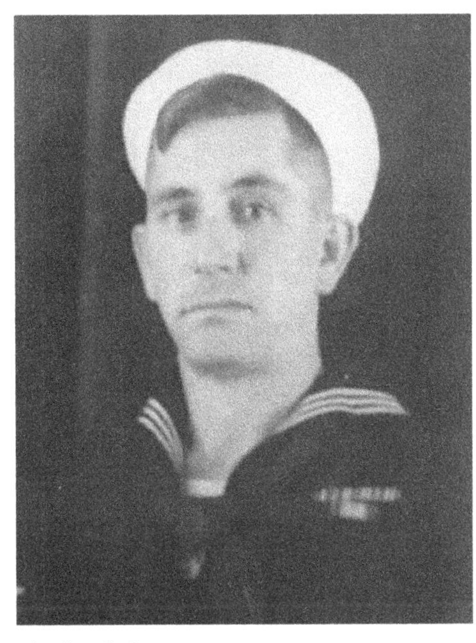

Floyd Soderberg.

11

Building on the Gunflint Trail

During World War II, Carl Soderberg wrote to his brother Floyd that government lots were now being offered for sale on the Gunflint Trail. Both brothers decided that this would be the perfect time to fulfill their dream. Floyd purchased one and a half government lots on Birch Lake, while Carl and his wife, Elinor, used war bonds to purchase 250 feet of lake shore on Poplar Lake. The brothers were thrilled to finally own property in what is now considered the "mid-Gunflint Trail" area; and better yet, the properties were only five miles apart.

Although the Soderberg brothers were finally ready to build, Floyd and Carl each had a different vision of how to best use their land. After the war, Floyd accepted a wonderful position as a carpet layer for Marshall Field & Company in Chicago. He decided that until he was able to retire, Birch Lake would have to remain a place to spend vacations. Carl, on the other hand, felt that his land could provide a good business opportunity and began to make plans for building rental cabins.

The Gunflint Trail—Its History and Opportunities

Originally, the Gunflint Trail was part of the ancestral lands of the Anishinaabe and Ojibwe people. Although the trail began as a simple footpath, it eventually grew into a winter snowshoe and dog team route from Gunflint Lake to a Native American village on Lake Superior.

Silver Creek Cliff.

With the advent of mining and logging during the late 1800s, sections of "tote" roads were built wide enough to accommodate oxen and wagons. These roads were used to access traplines or to carry freight to town. During the winter months, dog teams were still the mode for travel, and a trip from Grand Marais to Gunflint Lake usually took two days.

Near the end of World War I, with the establishment of the Superior National Forest, people became more interested in travel and outdoor recreation. Early residents Charlie and Petra Boostrom of Clearwater Lake were ahead of the curve when they founded Clearwater Lodge in 1915. Edith and Gilbert Gilbertsen followed in 1920, starting a hunting and fishing resort on Greenwood Lake.

As motorized vehicles became more common, in 1916, a rough automobile road was completed from Grand Marais to an area eight miles up the Gunflint Trail known as "the Pines" (a grove of old-growth pines untouched by logging). In 1922, this road was extended another twenty miles up the trail to Poplar and Hungry Jack lakes.

The new road reached Gunflint Lake in 1924, and then, five years later, Seagull Lake, where it ended. Concurrently, lodges and resorts began to follow. In 1928, Mae Spunner and her daughter Justine (Kerfoot) purchased a fishing camp (Gunflint Lodge) from Dora Blankenburg on Gunflint Lake.

By the 1930s, several mid-trail lodges were also established. On Hungry Jack Lake, Jesse Gapen built Gateway Hungry Jack Lodge. On Poplar Lake, Paul and Jennie Stolz, along with Wally and Helen Anderson, built

View of Grand Marais.

Rockwood Lodge. Also on Poplar Lake, Doc Rempel, a Russian immigrant who had worked in the CCC camps as a physician, built Old Northwoods Lodge (now White Pine Lodge), and Balsam Grove (now Nor'wester Lodge) was founded by Alis and Carl Brandt.

Interestingly, in 1930 to 1931, a toll road was built at the end of the Gunflint Trail to Saganaga Lake and the Chik-Wauk area by property owners Russell Blankenburg and Art Nunstedt.

A Gateway to the Wilderness

After three hundred years, the Gunflint Trail is no longer a mere footpath or a rough primitive road. Today, this fifty-seven-mile route has become a paved, two-lane National Scenic Byway that twists and winds elegantly through the Superior National Forest. It begins on the north shore of Lake Superior in Grand Marais and ends at Saganaga Lake, which is a large access point to the Boundary Waters Canoe Area Wilderness (BW-CAW), near the US–Ontario border.

By traveling the Gunflint Trail, a first-time visitor can easily access lodges, campgrounds, and outfitters. Just off the trail, there are scenic overlooks, hiking trails, and boat launches for inland lakes. Even a casual drive up the trail can offer sightings of wildlife such as moose, wolves, lynx, black bears, fox, and bald eagles.

BWCAW

The BWCAW (Boundary Waters Canoe Area Wilderness) is a protected 1.1-million-acre wilderness region within the northern third of the Superior National Forest. It is under the administration of the US Forest Service. This roadless, motorless wilderness can be accessed through many entrances on the Gunflint Trail. Within the BWCAW, an adventurous traveler can choose from two thousand or more designated campsites, over twelve hundred miles of canoe routes, more than a thousand lakes, and a variety of major hiking trails.

Memories of Traveling on the Old Gunflint Trail

From the mid-1940s to the early 1960s, every July my parents and I would spend two or more weeks at my uncle Floyd's cabin on Birch Lake. During the early years, the Gunflint Trail was still a work in progress and was unpaved. In fact, just driving from Chicago to Minnesota was challenging as there were no superhighways. Consequently, my father, mother, and I would leave Chicago on a Friday evening and drive all night through Wisconsin to Minnesota on slow, two-lane roads. At times, our trip would be further delayed if we followed a long military convoy. If we were lucky, by sunrise we would reach Duluth, where we would take a catnap in the car overlooking the Duluth Harbor.

In the early days, many North Shore visitors can probably recall the beauty of driving along the cliffs of Lake Superior on Highway 61 and then arriving in Grand Marais, only to face the roller-coaster hills and jutting rocks of the Gunflint Trail. As we drove onto this unpaved, gravel and dirt road, dust would billow out of the vents in the front seat of our car. Unfortunately, those jutting rocks could puncture the undercarriage of a car. I recall one year when our car leaked oil all the way up to Birch Lake. Our trip was especially difficult for my mother, Eva, as she suffered greatly from car sickness. Eva would practically kiss the ground when we would arrive, thirty-five miles later, at the cabin.

12

Carl—The Soderberg Cabins

My uncle, Carl Soderberg, began building rental cabins on the Gunflint Trail in 1945. His goal was to have two small cabins along the shore of Poplar Lake, with a home and a larger rental cabin across the trail amid a forest of pines. It was decided that during this building phase, Carl's wife, Elinor, would stay behind in Chicago until their daughter Carlene finished grade school in 1947.

Carl was a wonderful carpenter and craftsman. His finished cabins were all v-jointed, knotty pine. They had tile floors and even French windows with little panes of glass. Carl built all the cabinetry and even some of the furnishings. He would go into the woods and find a tree with just the right diameter and cut it down to make bed posts. He even found two trees with the same unusual "C" curvature which marked the entranceway to the main cabin office. Since the Soderberg Cabins offered a "housekeeping plan," each cabin included a sink, gas stove, and icebox.

Chik-Wauk Museum and Nature Center has a copy of Carlene's memoirs regarding her life on the Gunflint Trail. It is interesting to read about a wilderness life from the perspective of a young girl. Like her father, Carlene adored living in the woods, but readily admits that it was a "rough" way of life. The earliest photo I have of Carlene depicts her sitting on the stairs of Clearwater Lodge in 1936. She was only two years old. It wasn't long after that Carl began teaching her how use a "drop line" to bring fish into the boat hand-over-hand.

Carlene Soderberg, age 2, on the steps of Clearwater Lodge—1936.

By the 1940s, some of the larger lodges on the Gunflint Trail had generators, but a small operation like the Soderberg Cabins did not. Their business adventure began without plumbing, running water, electricity, or telephone. At night, they heated their home with an oilstove. Wood was free; therefore, propane gas was used sparingly—only for light and some cooking. At first, Carl installed woodstoves in all the rental cabins, but after one fisherman almost set the cabin on fire, he took them out.

Carl's wife, Elinor, may have been a city girl, but she was not afraid of hard work or of going without the usual conveniences. Upon arrival, Elinor varnished all the cabins and made curtains and feather ticks for comforters on an old treadle sewing machine. She was a good businesswoman and keen hostess. Elinor made sure that every new guest had their preference of drinking water (well, lake, or spring) in a crock on the cabin counter, and ice in the icebox. Guests were also offered trips to the garbage dump on Hungry Jack Lake to see bears, or given lessons on to how to fillet a fish.

Carlene commented that besides scouring outhouses and cleaning cabins, Elinor made her own bread, butchered deer, and preserved berries, fish, and venison for the winter. She wrote, "Mom washed all the linens and towels in washtubs of cold water with a scrub board. She did so much laundry her knuckles would bleed and her back would hurt. We would carry buckets of water up from the lake and pour them into two washtubs so Mom could do the wash. Dad put up aluminum lines for the laundry so they would not sag with the heavy sheets and blankets. If it rained, the sheets were hung on coat hangers from the ceiling. We did not have a washing

The Soderberg cabin known as the "Dollhouse."

machine. The second year, we were able to purchase a Maytag gasoline motor-driven ringer washing machine. It made Mom's work a lot easier."[25]

Carlene Soderberg— Boarding for High School

Carlene faced many challenges in her new life too. Grand Marais High School included grades one to twelve, and since the school bus only went as far as Maple Hill, it was necessary for her to board in town. Each year, the county did its best to place students in appropriate homes.

Soderberg Cabins main entrance.

Carlene's freshman year was not particularly fun. Carlene found it difficult to be separated from her family, and this became a time of "adjustment and turmoil." That year, Carlene stayed with two different families, and her parents found it necessary to rent a cabin in Grand Marais twice.

Carlene and Carl.

Thankfully, things turned around. During Carlene's sophomore year, she boarded with Sandy and Reba Gilchrist, and had her own bedroom. The Gilchrists owned a big house on Main Street across from the break wall. Carlene still remembers them as being "the nicest people you would ever want to know."

After school, Carlene often stopped for cherry cokes at Lang's Fountain, where she would look for the latest issue of Seventeen magazine. Her father, Carl, would try to drive to town every week and bring Carlene home for the weekends. When he couldn't come, Carlene would stand outside the post office and plead for a ride with Don Brazell, the freight and mail carrier.

The First Christmas

Carlene's first Christmas on the Gunflint Trail was magical. In order to make things festive, Carl went out and chopped down a large tree. They used the top part of the tree to decorate for Christmas and cut up the rest for firewood. Since there was no electricity, Elinor found some candle holders that could be clipped onto the branches. When the tree was completely lit with candles, Carlene was thrilled, and exclaimed, "How exciting." Carl, on the other hand, said, "How dangerous." Although the tree, whenever lit, was beautiful, the family had to stand right by the tree to watch that it did not catch on fire. The next year, Carl purchased a string of Christmas lights and hooked them up to a car battery that he set behind the back of the tree. (Carlene preferred the candles.)

Elinor and Carl next to the ice house.

A Christmas break from school was not just a time for a holiday celebration. More importantly, it was a time to harvest ice. Carl would measure the depth of the ice on Poplar Lake regularly until it reached a certain thickness. When he was satisfied, he would begin cutting a chosen field of ice with a saw. This work was a family effort.

After the ice was cut, Elinor's job was to hold tightly onto Carl as he lifted the large blocks of ice out of the lake with ice tongs. At this point, Carlene would help her parents push and pull each block into an icehouse that Carl had built on their property near the shore of the lake. Once the ice blocks were stacked, Carlene was in charge of packing sawdust around and on top of each block. The sawdust acted as insulation and kept the ice frozen all summer. During the summer, this ice was used for refrigeration and to "gussy up" guests' drinks.

Each month was filled with many activities and challenges. Carl trapped beaver and fisher, and would hang the cured hides on the cabins. In the winter, the family used snowshoes and skis while backpacking, and to maneuver in the deep snow. When temperatures dropped to forty degrees below zero, often the car would not start. As a remedy, Carl would put fuel oil in a pan, light it, and place it under the engine block. It worked every time.

Women in the Wilderness

In those days, women and girls knew how to handle a gun and always carried a hunting knife in a sheath on their belt. In her booklet of Gunflint Trail memories, Carlene wrote, "We always had guns. In fact, my mother slept with a German Luger under her pillow. My father taught her how to use it. My mom and I were not afraid because my dad knew just what to do in every situation, whether hunting, fishing, trapping, canoeing, camping, or hiking. He knew how to survive in the wilderness. He was my hero and protector."

In the fall, Carlene would often go partridge hunting on her bike, carrying a rifle across the handlebars. She would also help Carl hunt deer. Carlene would stand on a stump as her dad drove deer to her.

When they shot a deer, Carl would gut it and skin it. Together, they would find a way to get the carcass home, where Elinor would cut it up into smaller portions. The venison was wrapped in wax paper and sometimes put on a table in one of the cabins where it would freeze solid. Nothing was ever wasted.

Carlene was given a great amount of freedom in the woods. She became a good canoeist and portaged into many Boundary Water lakes with her family and friends. Rose Lake was her favorite. She loved to swim in Poplar Lake, and even tried log rolling.

Porcupines were plentiful and a nuisance in those days. Carl told her if she ever became lost in the woods, she should club a porcupine and eat it. Carl also taught Carlene how to set up minnow traps in a floating bog area, using white bread and eggshells. She tried to remember to pump the minnow pail on her way back to the road. Otherwise, she would arrive home with dead minnows.

Carl Soderberg

Carl was an impressive man. Physically, he was extremely handsome and fit. Many people remarked that he looked like the movie star Randolph

Scott. But what was even more impressive was his knowledge and ability to live off the land.

Soderberg Cabins was Carl's labor of love. Besides building and maintaining the cabins, the property also needed his special care. Every spring, Carl had to redo the dock. There was a crib at the end of the dock filled with rocks which he anchored at the other end into the embankment with logs and more rock. As the ice thawed in the spring, the ice and water from the long sweep of the lake would twist and turn and damage the crib.

Carl guiding for Dave Clark.

Carl also built a beach for his guests. He cleaned the bottom of the lake around the dock so people could go swimming without encountering leeches or stubbing their toes on rocks. For easy access to the beach and dock, Carl built stairs down to the lake, first with wood and later with stone.

One year, Carl visited my family in Chicago and told us about a scare he'd had that winter working deep in the woods. While he was checking his traplines, a large pack of wolves passed on a ridge nearby. Carl said he felt he owed his safety to the fact that he had been downwind from the pack. (Today many people feel that wolves will not attack a man; but years ago, many folks feared wolves—especially during the long winter months when wolves were hungry or hunting in a pack.)

After the first winter on the Gunflint Trail, Carl and Elinor realized that even though their rental business was successful, a small seasonal business would not be sufficient to meet their needs. Therefore, Carl began working as a guide for Dave Clark at Rockwood Lodge, and as a carpenter with Emerson Morris building cabins. Emerson, who later was elected as the sheriff of Cook County, had been a bush pilot and owned a seaplane.

Emerson Morris picking up Carl for work.

Every morning, Emerson would pull up to the Soderberg dock with his plane and pick up Carl to go to work.

Elinor Soderberg

As the Soderbergs contemplated a second winter on the Gunflint Trail, Carl and Elinor decided that it would help financially if Carl found work in the Twin Cities. That meant Elinor would have to spend the winter alone at the cabin, since Carlene would be boarding in town for school. Of course, without a car, electricity, phone, or running water, Elinor would have to face months of isolation and physical hardship.

According to Carlene, Elinor was snowed in for at least two weeks at a time, as the plow was not always able to get through. For a petite woman, Elinor was very strong. That was a good thing, as during that winter it became necessary to shovel one path to the biffy and another to the lake on a regular basis. In order to get water, Elinor had to chop a hole through several inches of ice on the lake. Afterwards, while carrying buckets of water back up the hill to the cabin, she found that those buckets became heavier and heavier as they picked up snow.

Baking bread was another challenge. Without warmth, dough will not rise. As a solution, Elinor put the dough in a large washbasin, covered it

Elinor chopping though ice.

with a dish towel, and then hung it from hooks high in the rafters. Carlene remarked that her mother never complained and doesn't know how she ever made it through that long winter. Surely, there must have been times of great loneliness, as mail delivery was only once a week, and the few neighbors lived miles apart. Perhaps one saving grace was that Elinor liked to sew and knit. She also had a small radio that sat atop a battery that was three times its size. However, even in good weather, the deposits of ore in the area caused such bad reception that the radio only worked at night.

Sometimes the Wilderness Wins

By 1949, Carl and Elinor realized they could not maintain their beloved business. Sadly, Elinor and Carlene moved back to Chicago where Carlene finished high school. Although Carl and Elinor eventually divorced, Carlene's heart remained on the Gunflint Trail. The summer she graduated from high school (1951), Carlene took a bus to Grand Marais and reopened the Soderberg Cabin rental business all by herself. Carl had remained on the trail and supplemented those good intentions. Yet, even with all her hard work, by summer's end Carlene returned to Chicago.

Joyce and Carlene.

In 1955, Elinor and Carlene attempted to reopen the cabin business one more time. Regrettably, in the end, they reached the conclusion that the business would never be self-sustaining. Floyd Soderberg tried to keep the family's dream alive and purchased the cabins. He held onto the property until the mid-1960s. (Today, the cabins are gone, and all that remains are the icehouse and the stone stairway down to the lake.)

The Call of the Wild

Perhaps Jack London was right, and there really is a "call of the wild." I know my mother's family, the Soderbergs, heard that call and could not be satisfied in life until they answered it. I believe many people who live on the Gunflint Trail (past and present) feel the same way. They would prefer to hold a combination of jobs rather than leave the wilderness and the special kind of freedom it offers. Even the great adventurer Teddy Roosevelt wrote, "The farther one gets into the wilderness, the greater is the attraction of its lonely freedom." Roosevelt felt hardship and risk were two key components of what he termed the "strenuous life."

After the loss of his business, Carl continued living on the Gunflint Trail. Eventually, he purchased another piece of property on Poplar Lake, not far from Trail Center. He began a small trapping business with Harry Nolan, who ran Hungry Jack Outfitters, and worked as both a fishing and hunting guide. In the winters, he returned to Chicago and worked as a carpenter.

13

Floyd's Birch Lake Cabin

Birch Lake is one of the smaller lakes on the Gunflint Trail. Although it is fairly narrow in width, it is about three and a half miles long, and its deepest point is seventy feet. In the 1940s, the lake was located a good distance from the Gunflint Trail. (The early Gunflint Trail ran west of the current trail.) Therefore, Carl helped Floyd survey and build a spur route from the old Gunflint Trail down to the site where Floyd had chosen to build his cabin. (Later, in 1963 to 1964, the Gunflint Trail was realigned and brought alongside the length of Birch Lake. In fact, today Birch Lake is the site of a designated overlook. It highlights the start of the Laurentian Divide, where the water on Birch Lake flows north to Hudson Bay, rather than south to the Gulf of Mexico.)

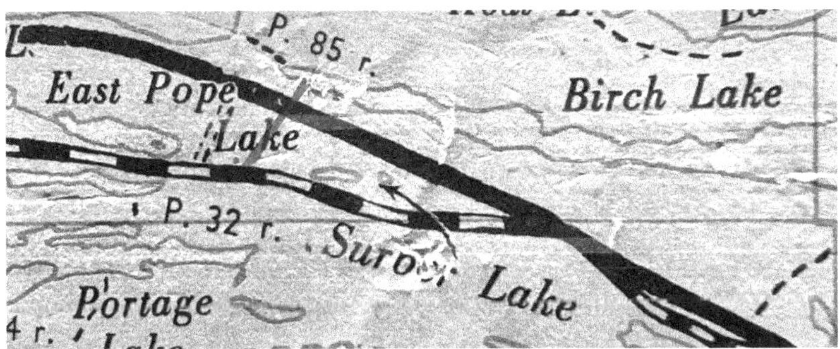

The broken line is the location of the old Gunflint Trail. The perpendicular line crossing the current Gunflint Trail notes the location of the spur road to Birch Lake and Floyd's cabin.

Trappers Harry Nolan and Carl Soderberg.

A Bear/Bare Story

My first trip to Birch Lake was in 1948, and I was eight years old. That summer, I played and watched as my uncle Floyd began to build his cabin. Since the building site was located deep in the wilderness, I could not help but feel a keen sense of excitement and uncertainty—especially when I was sternly warned not to wander away from the campsite. Yet, the reason I remember the cabin building time so vividly is that it was my first sighting of a bear.

As I recall, our camp consisted of several tents near Floyd's chosen building site. My grandfather Charlie, uncles Carl and Floyd, and my father, George Cleaver, were all part of the building team. At night, my mother and I opted to sleep more comfortably in the car. One night, our sleep was interrupted by gunfire and all kinds of commotion.

When my mother turned the car lights on, we were shocked to see Charlie standing in the headlights wielding his rifle at a huge, angry bear that was towering on his hind feet above him. Later, we learned that the bear had ripped off the corner of my grandfather Charlie's tent, just missing his head as he was sleeping. As frightening as this scene was to an eight-year-old child, it was also very funny as my grandfather was only

Early tents.

wearing his long underwear with the back flap down—revealing another kind of bare.

Hidden History in the Woods

I believe it was that same summer when my father took me on a trek to see the vestiges of an old logging camp on the north side of Birch Lake. Hidden within the undergrowth of the woods was an abandoned, deteriorating mess hall where dinner plates were still sitting on one of the long dining tables.

Author Joyce Cleaver (Leddy).

Unfortunately, throughout the years I have never been able to relocate that structure. In fact, I had begun to think this story was a figment of my imagination until early Mayhew Lake resident Roy Carlson told me that he remembered it too. Even today there are still many indications that logging camps once existed within the deep woods near Birch and Mayhew Lakes. One can find rusted-out old cars, horse collars, and even the remnants of railroad beds.

Floyd's cabin on Birch Lake—1940s.

A Good Fish Story

I believe the building of the Birch Lake cabin went on into a second and possibly third year as I have memories that include other people and events. It was during this time when Floyd's new lady friend and her thirteen-year-old son, Leo, joined the group. Mable Greenly Voss was originally from Sandstone, and, as I understand, became part owner of the cabin.

My uncle Floyd was a rather small, lean man with lively energy and great charm. He loved kids and couldn't wait to teach Leo about the woods and how to fish. One afternoon, we saw Leo furiously rowing back to the campsite, calling for help. He yelled out that he thought he had caught a large fish and it had broken his line. Somehow, Leo managed to tie the broken line to the back of the boat and began rowing at top speed.

Of course, everyone doubted that this young, inexperienced boy had caught a fish. They assured him that he had most likely snagged a log. When Leo reached the shore, Floyd patiently waded out into the lake. As he dug deep down into the water, we all fully expected him to bring up part of a tree. To everyone's amazement, Floyd instead came up with a giant northern pike.

Unfortunately, we never had a chance to dine on this trophy fish. That night, Floyd had a gallbladder attack and was driven to a hospital in Duluth. The next time we looked into the live-box, we found the fish dead. It became my father's and my task to row across Birch Lake and bury the putrid fish.

The Finished Cabin

Floyd's cabin was the first cabin built on Birch Lake, and it consisted of one room with an outhouse behind the building. The décor was sparse. There were two bunk beds, a picnic table, and a small kitchen area with a red pump, sink, gas stove, and an old-fashioned icebox. Down by the lake, there was a small wooden dock with a live-box for fish. Floyd also had his US Navy hammock fastened between two birch trees. Although there was nothing fancy about the cabin or property, to me it held a whole world of wonder and fun.

Eva, George and Joyce Cleaver.

In the very beginning, my mother, father, and I would spend our July vacation weeks completely isolated and alone at the cabin. (Until he retired, Floyd usually stayed at Birch Lake during the month of August. He would also find time to drive up for fishing openers and hunting with his brother Carl in the fall.)

As I mentioned, it was not easy to access Floyd's cabin from the old Gunflint Trail. The spur route that Carl built (where the power lines come down today), was particularly rough and difficult to travel—especially when there was any amount of rain.

In good weather, we could take the spur route all the way down to the cabin; but once it rained, we found that the ground turned into a slick, oily substance, and invariably our car would get stuck in the mud. Consequently, we began to use the spur route only to drive as far as where the current Gunflint Trail is located today. After parking the car, we would backpack our groceries and suitcases the rest of the way down the hill.

The Drowley's boat house.

Isolation in the Woods

As a child, I loved the isolation and remoteness of Floyd's cabin. It was a completely different lifestyle from my home on the outskirts of Chicago. Yet living deep within a dense forest, without a good road or any form of communication, could be sobering. During the day, I could sense that animals were all around. Unfortunately, my mother never held back from warning me on how easy it was for bears to break into cabins. She even knew a woman who spent several hours in an outhouse while surrounded by a pack of wolves.

I grew to have a healthy respect for all wildlife. Of course, I loved the calls of the loons, deer sightings, and the slapping sounds of beaver tails. But at night, it was not unusual for bears to rub up against the side of our cabin, or to hear howls from a pack of wolves on nearby Moss Lake. I learned to always be alert. In time, I could even recognize the sound of porcupines when they rattled their quills. Our dog Tippy was not as alert, and once returned home with his snout full of quills.

During those early years, Birch Lake was filled with walleye and northern pike. Since we believed that walleye fed in the evening, we would go fishing from 6:30 to 9:30 p.m. We would usually catch our limit. Once we entered the cabin, my job was to record how many fish were caught and by whom. Those numbers were written on a pine board hung next to the door. Most often, my mother took the prize.

In the evenings, we would make popcorn or fudge and play cards and board games by the light of kerosene lanterns. When the mantles of those lanterns began to turn orange and wane, my dad would declare that it was time for bed. This usually happened way too early, in my opinion.

"Frenchy" and Betsy the Bear.

The 1950s—Changes on Birch Lake

One summer when we arrived at the cabin, I looked across the lake to see a newly built boathouse just to the west. I remember being shocked and angered that other people had discovered my secret lake and retreat in the woods. In fact, the boathouse, which still stands today, was built by the Drowley family, who had begun a logging and sawmill operation not far from Birch Lake.

Mr. and Mrs. Drowley built a cabin high on the north side of the lake where they lived with their daughter Marian. Another smaller cabin was built closer to the boathouse and was where Mr. Dowley's chief foreman—a French Canadian called "Frenchy"—stayed. Our first introduction to Frenchy was when he went motoring down Birch Lake with his pet bear, Betsy, sitting in the front seat. (This was well before the Hamm's Beer commercial with Sasha the bear.)

I believe the Drowley family lived on Birch Lake for only a couple of years. Even though I was distraught that someone else had the nerve to build on my private lake, in a short time I became friends with Marian Drowley. I felt very grown up when Marian invited me to go fishing with

Joyce with Marian and an unknown child.

her. On those fishing trips, I tried not to let on that I was squeamish about putting minnows on my own hook. Marian and I became pen pals for a while after I returned to Chicago.

A Frightening Experience

Around 1951, I had one of my most frightening experiences. I was about eleven years old and was playing with a large birch log down by the dock. All of a sudden, I heard my mother scream from Floyd's cabin on the hill. I turned around to see a bear charging down the hill directly at me. When the bear and I were practically eyeball to eyeball—and I was faced with his pig-like snout and garbage breath—I instinctively raised the birch log up in a threatening gesture. To my surprise, the bear immediately screeched to a halt. He then reeled around and ran straight up a tree.

It didn't take long for us to realize that the bear was not a "he" but a "she"—Betsy, the pet bear from across the lake. No doubt somewhere in her training, Betsy had been beaten. When I raised the log as a weapon, she stopped dead in her tracks. It was easy to forgive Betsy as the log must have appeared to be a fish. Unfortunately, I have had a great fear of bears ever since.

Friends and Family Visit Birch Lake

During the 1950s, other family members and friends began to join us at Floyd's cabin. Helen Soderberg Heinecke (my mother's sister), her husband Earl and daughter Andrene were regular guests and were particularly great fun. Earl was an artist with a delightful sense of humor. I still have a home movie he produced at the cabin. The film starred my mother who was urgently knocking on the door of an occupied outhouse. Each time she would knock, another person would open the door and come out. There must have been about ten different individuals who responded to my mother's insistent knocking. These even included my dog Tippy and my eighty-year-old grandfather Charlie, who now walked with a cane. I still laugh whenever I watch a copy of that video today.

My father's sister Carol's family took less to the woods. As I recall, Carol's husband had a particularly hard time with bugs. One year, he showed up with a special concoction he had made that was guaranteed to keep all insects away. Unfortunately, after slathering this solution all over his body, he became so bitten by mosquitos their family had to abandon their vacation and drive home.

Aspen Annie

Sometime in the 1950s, after his divorce, my uncle Carl had a romance with Annie Heffner (Anna Olena Gladen), who was the owner and proprietor of Aspen Lake Lodge. "Aspen Annie" was one of the more colorful people who lived on the Gunflint Trail. Annie ran a popular saloon at Aspen Lake Lodge and rented cabins. In a talk given for the Gunflint Trail Historical Society in 2022, Steve Blumke, who had interviewed her family and knew her from when he was a young boy, characterized Annie as a cross between Kitty from Gunsmoke and Mae West.

As background, it appears that Annie did not have an easy life. She was born with a cleft lip and grew up on a hard-working farm. In the 1930s, Annie married Fred Heffner, a World War I vet who walked with a limp. Sometime after their marriage, Annie and Fred moved onto his family's considerable-sized property on Clearwater Lake. Shortly thereafter, the young couple began to hand-build log cabins with the intention to start a resort. In 1942, as a way to supplement their income, Annie and Fred worked as managers of the Arrowhead Hotel in Grand Marais. During the 1940s, Fred also took out several mortgages and loans. The largest mortgage was taken in 1949.

On October 2, 1949, Fred mysteriously disappeared after telling his brother Andrew, who lived on the property, that he was going to walk to the Gunflint Trail to pick up the mail. He was expecting a government disability check.

According to the October 6 Cook County News Herald, the distance from the resort to the trail was about two miles. It was believed that because of Fred's lameness, it was unlikely that he would walk that distance. However, he did not take the car. Sheriff Malner commented that Fred had not been seen since he reached the Clearwater Road, which was about six hundred feet from the resort.

Aspen Annie, Eva, and Helen.

By October 27, the authorities admitted that, even after a massive hunt, they had lost hope of finding Fred alive and now suspected foul play. Annie and Andrew were told that they were not above suspicion.

In 1953, at Floyd's cabin, I met Aspen Annie when Carl began dating her and wanted to introduce her to my family. To make her feel welcome, my mother invited Annie to join us on a day trip to Port Arthur and Fort William (Thunder Bay), Canada. (My parents knew Annie's sister Hazel and her husband Eddie Giroux, who had been a trapper on Poplar Lake).

I have to admit that as a young teen, I had heard the stories about Annie's missing husband and was a bit apprehensive to meet her. But, as I recall, we had a lovely day and picnicked along the way. Even my aunt Helen and grandpa Charlie, who now lived with us, came along.

In retrospect, I realize now that it must have been terribly hard for Annie to constantly face suspicion or speculation about her husband Fred and his disappearance. I understand that Annie lived in constant fear that if Fred had actually fallen victim to foul play, perhaps she was not safe either. Annie was not even sure she could trust Fred's brother, who had mental challenges. Fred was never found, and the mystery has never been solved.

To her credit, Annie remained on the Gunflint Trail and went on to make Aspen Lake Lodge and its saloon into a successful business. Interestingly, up until Fred's disappearance, Annie had never taken a drop of alcohol.

Roy Carlson, who originally came to the Gunflint Trail with the CCC camps and built the first cabin on Mayhew Lake, told me that he and his wife Rose loved going to the Aspen Lake Lodge during its heyday. Roy said that Annie was a good hostess and offered a great place on the trail for

Joyce, George, Annie, Eva, and Charlie (back).

people to meet, congregate, and have fun.

I never saw Annie again as the relationship with my uncle did not last.

Eva, Carl, and Floyd Soderberg

In the late 1950s, during spring, Carl and Floyd invited my mother, Eva, to join them at Birch Lake for one of their camping adventures. Honestly, I think they wanted her along for her cooking and fishing skills—but Eva adored her bothers and the woods, so if there was an ulterior motive, it never bothered her.

On that trip, Eva won the fishing prize again when she snagged a double-headed axe from the bottom of Rose Lake. Because the axe was quite old, Floyd and Carl believed it had been used by the voyageurs in the 1700s. Unfortunately, since this relic was so heavy, they decided to leave it behind. Carl safely stashed it away in a bear's cave somewhere near Rose Lake. He planned to return one day to retrieve it, but I don't think he ever did.

14

Eva Soderberg— Trail Service Center

While growing up in Chicago, every Sunday my uncle Floyd would come for dinner. That meant I listened to tales of the Gunflint Trail every week for twenty years. By the 1960s, not only was Floyd making plans to retire on Birch Lake, but he also spent a good amount of time trying to convince his friends and my parents that they should retire there too.

Floyd was a very generous man and gifted some of his property to a few special friends. This included his surrogate sons Gene Doody and Leo Voss. Gene Doody eventually built a cabin on this property, where he and his wife Rita later lived full time. In fact, Gene became a popular figure both in Grand Marais and on the Gunflint Trail when he opened a carpet business in the building where the Cook County Herald offices are located today.

I graduated from college and married in the summer of 1962. Facing an empty nest, my parents decided to follow Floyd's advice. My dad took an early retirement from Lehman Bros in Chicago and purchased Trail Service Center. Carl and Floyd loved the idea as Floyd was due to retire from Marshall Fields in 1965. The three Soderberg siblings were excited to be reunited once again—all living on the Gunflint Trail.

George Flavel and the Cleavers.

The Early History of Trail Service Center

The property of Trail Service Center (known now as Trail Center Lodge) has always had an ideal location. Built on Poplar Lake, it sits right on the Gunflint Trail, about halfway between Grand Marais and Canada. Originally, in 1938, the Trail Service Center building was part of a sawmill and logging camp run by Sam and Mayme Seppala. According to the Seppalas' daughter, Gladys, after the mill was established, it "flourished, operating twenty-four hours a day with one hundred men."

Gladys recalled that the main building (Trail Service Center) was located a little way from the camp. At that time, the building operated as a store and their home. The store was in the front part of the building and offered "supplies, a bar, and two nickel slot machines. The Seppalas slept in a room in the back while Gladys slept in the loft."[22]

The mill fell on tough times in 1940, and closed that year. Tragically, Sam Seppala drowned on July 4, 1940. He had been in a canoe that day wearing heavy wool pants, a wool shirt, and boots—no life jacket. In her remembrances, Gladys noted that her father was not a good swimmer.

Trail Service Center sat empty for several years until Bev Johnson purchased the building. My cousin Carlene knew the Johnsons and remembers a kitchen in the front of the building to the right of the main door, but she does not believe the family lived in the building as they had another cabin close by. The Johnsons owned the building only a short time, as Bev's wife ran the Trading Post on Main Street in Grand Marais. She preferred living in town. Bev sold the building to George Flavell in 1948.

I still remember my first visit to Trail Service Center, which must have been shortly after George Flavell's purchase. My father needed some sup-

Postcard shows the house behind Trail Service Center.

plies and took me along as an eight-year-old girl. I felt intimidated when surrounded by several large, wild-looking loggers and fishermen. I couldn't help but think these men looked a lot scarier than the bears.

George Flavell was always a helpful, cordial man to my family. My dad counted on George whenever he needed supplies, advice, or to purchase another Lazy Ike—supposedly the best fishing lure for walleyes. From 1948 to 1962, my family was witness to many of the improvements George Flavell made to Trail Service Center. We thought he was particularly innovative when he built a small motel.

New Ownership—The Cleavers

By purchasing Trail Service Center, my parents took on a huge endeavor—"service" was certainly the name of the business. At the end of the summer of 1963, my husband Tom and I spent a few weeks staying with my parents at Trail Service Center before heading to Fort Bliss, Texas, where Tom was to fulfill his service as a Second Lieutenant in the US Army. Judging from the amount of weight my parents had lost, we could see that the resort business was not an easy task.

Eva and George lived in a small house, which is gone today. It was lakeside, just behind Trail Service Center. I don't think they spent much

Mootsie and Albert.

Eva and George.

time in that house as they worked twenty-four/seven. These inexperienced, older Chicagoans jumped right in and began operating a grocery store, bar, motel, and cabins. They also rented canoes, and sold gas and live bait. If that was not enough, George decided to open a small restaurant with simple fare in the bar area—mostly hamburgers with or without fried onions and chips. They charged fifty cents for a cheeseburger and forty cents for plain. More surprising, Dad installed a machine for slicing cold meat in the grocery store. He wanted to create a deli.

A Bit Overwhelmed

Tom and I tried to help my parents while we stayed with them. We learned how to properly fry hamburgers for the guests and how to patiently remain behind the bar late into the evening until the last person left—around midnight. Sleep hours were short for my parents as it was not unusual for fishermen to knock on their cabin door by five a.m. if they needed bait.

Unfortunately, Eva and George thought keeping long hours and never saying "no" was the only way to successfully operate a short, seasonal business. Thank goodness one day I had the courage to say "no" to a group of fishermen who arrogantly threw a mess of fish on the bar and demanded that I clean and fry them right then for their supper.

Mootsie, a woman of short stature, became my mother's savior when she tried to find someone to help clean cabins. Mootsie was born in a logging camp and had seen it all. She and her husband, Albert, worked as loggers and lived in a shack in the woods. Mootsie was a hard worker and found ingenious ways to overcome her shortness.

In a short time, Trail Service Center blossomed. It also became a well-known place on the Gunflint Trail to gather and have fun. Like Aspen Lake Lodge, some evenings E. J. Croft played ragtime on the piano while wearing his leather "choppers." I've also been told that today's owners of Nor'wester Lodge, Luana and Carl Brandt, visited Trail Service Center while they were dating. Senator Mondale's daughter and her bodyguards visited too. In June 1964, Eva and one of her employees, Mary Joe Retzer, even came to the aid of a woman who had just given birth to a baby en route from Saganaga Lake to Grand Marais. While in the parking lot, they helped the new mother prepare for the rest of the trip to the hospital in Grand Marais. Justine Kerfoot later wrote in her column, "The Cleavers of Trail Service Center are noted for their ability to meet all challenges and take care of all customers."

Tom's first trip to the Northwoods was in 1963. I taught him how to run a boat motor and introduced him to canoeing, portaging, and real fishing. During our stay, we saw our first lynx and explored many lakes in my dad's canoe. The most exciting experience was portaging the Granite River. In fact, one of my parents' guests showed us the way.

Tony

While visiting my parents, we stayed in the motel. Truthfully, it was strange for me to realize that some of the furniture from my childhood home now adorned cabin rentals. Shortly after our arrival, we met a young man who was staying in the motel unit next door. He was a clean-cut looking guy, about eight years older than Tom and me. He drove a new Mercedes and claimed to be a barber from Chicago.

Somehow these facts didn't jive, and I was a bit suspicious. However, "Tony," as I will call him, had a jovial personality and was very engaging. He absolutely loved the Gunflint Trail and lamented that he had been away from the area far too long. On this trip, he wanted to catch up on all the things he missed.

Tony begged my husband to join him on a portage down the Granite River. Not knowing Tony, and concerned that Tom's new paddling skills would be severely tested, I decided to invite myself along. Although I had been a bit apprehensive, we had an amazing day and found Tony to be a wonderful fisherman and guide.

During the rest of the week, we joined Tony on several other fishing excursions. Tony even knocked on our motel door one morning and surprised us with a hot breakfast before one of our trips. He confided in us that he was divorced and missed his wife's family and their Italian cooking.

The night before Tony was to return home, we decided to thank him for his wonderful companionship. I made a big pot of Italian meatballs in Trail Service Center's kitchen and served him a farewell dinner in the restaurant. We were sad to say goodbye.

After we had moved to El Paso, my mother called one day and told us that she had received a visit from the FBI. They were seeking information about Tony. It seems that Tony had served time as a bank robber and was still under investigation as the stolen money had never been found. I believe mother said that he had been a part of some infamous gang.

15

The Wilderness—A Place for Common Ground

I love the words from a poem entitled "A Note from the Trail" by Amy Ludwig VanDerwater. One stanza speaks about the common ground one finds along a hiking trail in a wilderness: "All lives are equal when you find them here: poison ivy, bear, tick, human child."

I have traveled the Gunflint Trail for eighty-three years. It has taught me many lessons. Perhaps the greatest is that no matter who or what we think we are, we can find commonality within the primitive sanctity of the wilderness. The love of nature is a rallying point. Within the forests and on the lakes, we join forces. We meet, share stories, and trade skills that help us survive.

The Recluses

My family knew several people who lived on the Gunflint Trail who would have been considered recluses. In the 1940s, two men called Andy and Ernie lived a couple of hundred yards west of Trail Service Center. Ernie had a horse, and cut and sold pulpwood. My cousin Carlene remembers that Andy and Ernie each had their own separate shacks and lived only a few feet apart. Their life was very simple. One of the men only had light from a single kerosene lamp. In the evenings, all he would do was sit and stare at that one lamp.

Many people remember another reclusive man named Cyril. In the 1950s to 1960s, he lived in an eight-by-ten-foot shack about fifty feet

Ollar and Stephen.

west of Hungry Jack Road. For heat, he used a woodstove. If someone needed some odd jobs done, Cyril would be there. He was especially helpful to
Lydia Miller, a widow and long-time resident of Poplar Lake who had health
problems. My husband bought minnows from Cyril. Cyril even helped us
collect rock from Carlton Peak in order to build a fireplace. I remember him
being a man of few words.

Then there was Gorsky. When my parents owned Trail Service Center,
this man was down on his luck and began living in a car with his dog. When
he wanted companionship, Gorsky would come into the store and talk
about his sightings of UFOs. In a city, normally one would walk away from
these kinds of men. On the Gunflint Trail, they became part of our lives.

The Anonymous

Another man who was a bit of a loner but was always helpful to our
family, was Ollar Snevets. The rumor was that Ollar had moved into the
woods to escape a bad divorce or perhaps alimony payments. In the 1960s,
Ollar lived in a trailer across the trail, not far from Trail Service Center.

Ollar was a lumberjack. His truck was an old school bus with the body
sawed off. Carlene remembers Ollar as being very kind to her young son,
Stephen. She said he was a huge man in stature, and he seemed to wear his
long johns in both winter and summer.

Al Capone. John Dillinger. Tommy Banks. "Trenchcoat Robbers."

After he died, we learned that Ollar Snevets's real name was "Rallo Stevens." Wanting to be anonymous, Ollar had cleverly spelled his real name backwards.

The Mob

Ever since my father's experience of being at the Biograph Theatre the night John Dillinger was killed, he became fascinated with the actions of gangsters and the mafia. When I was a teenager, he told me there were even mob connections on the Gunflint Trail.

No doubt, my dad would have loved to have seen the 2019 Chik-Wauk Museum and Nature Center display on the gangster Tommy Banks and his relationship with local resident Billy Needham. My parents knew Billy, and admired his wonderful craftsmanship with diamond willow.

Tommy was a bootlegger who was involved with the Minneapolis mob during the 1930s and 1940s. He made a fortune bootlegging liquor to the Twin Cities from Canada during the prohibition. Today, some folks say there was a bootlegging trail from Canada down the old South Lake Trail that came out near Northwoods Lodge, which was on the Gunflint Trail at the time.

Tommy and his wife Reta built a cabin on Hungry Jack Lake in the mid-1930s. Interestingly, he had a hidden compartment in the original main cabin under a false floor, and the garage had living quarters for his bodyguards.

Billy took care of Tommy's cabin and was his fishing guide. Reportedly, Billy said that on his first fishing trip with Tommy, they took a large canoe to Rose Lake with several bodyguards. While fishing, someone in the party hooked a very large northern. After a long battle, they finally managed to bring the fish up to the canoe. However, upon seeing the size of the fish, Billy realized that it was too large to bring into the already crowded canoe. As he started to pull out his hunting knife in order to cut the fish loose, "… Tommy's bodyguards all drew out their pistols and dispatched the fish in a blast of bullets."[30]

Today, there are several websites and blogs that carry stories about notorious gangsters, bootleggers, and criminals who frequented the North Shore of Lake Superior during the 1920s and 30s. It seems these criminals found the wilderness of Minnesota to be a great "getaway" for some rest and relaxation. Al Capone, John Dillinger, and Baby Face Nelson all are names mentioned.

Al Capone purportedly spent time in Illgen City and at Lutsen. The Lutsen Resort has a wonderful story on its website about Al Capone paying twenty dollars in damages after leaving behind a bullet-riddled fish house that he had occupied during his stay. Local lore also says Al Capone was a frequent visitor to the original Naniboujou Social Club.

In the late 1990s, it was discovered that one of the infamous "Trench Coat Robbers" lived in Hovland (eighteen miles northeast of Grand Marais). William A. Kirkpatrick and his partner Ray A. Bowman had been robbing banks all over the United States, starting in 1982. It seems they avoided identification for fifteen years due to their precise and thorough planning. Their most famous heist was pulling off the largest bank robbery in US history. On February 10, 1997, they robbed a bank near Tacoma, Washington, netting $4,461,681 in cash. In fact, they were featured in an episode of Unsolved Mysteries in 1992, shedding light on their criminal activities.

16

Transitions—The 1960s

The 1950s brought electricity and plumbing to the Gunflint Trail. As a result, more and more families began to seek accommodations. By the 1960s, many lodges that had primarily catered to fishermen began upgrading their cabins to include kitchens, small bedrooms, and bathrooms with housekeeping plans. During this same time, the Gunflint Trail was improved and paved, at least as far as Trail Service Center. (The last section was completed in the late 1970s.)

My uncle Floyd was particularly happy when a large section of the Gunflint Trail was moved and brought down to run alongside Birch Lake. This realignment took place between late 1963 and early 1964, just in time for Floyd's retirement.

A New Wilderness Bill

The 1960s marked the onset of significant turmoil for resort and cabin owners. A new wilderness bill was introduced and passed that forced all property owners within the Boundary Waters to sell their properties to the government. The property owners were allowed to stay on their properties until they passed. This bill also gave the US Forest Service authority to curtail the use of motors on certain lakes, where they had previously been free to operate. Canoeists who used three-horse motors on larger border lakes were especially affected.

During that period, many cabin owners thought of "grandfathering" their properties just in case of potential removal of individual ownership near the Superior National Forest. Individuals from the Gunflint Trail

Carl Soderberg.

formed a group called Concerned Citizens of Cook County. Justine Kerfoot of Gunflint Lake made several trips to Washington to testify before Congressional Committees and contact congressmen. In 1964, the BWCAW received wilderness status, leading to stricter regulations compared to when my family first arrived on the Gunflint Trail.

Moving On

Suffice it to say that in their brief ownership of Trail Service Center, my parents embarked on a grand adventure. In the process, they learned that running a short-season, full-service business at their age was not only physically demanding, but also financially unpredictable. By 1966, they had sold Trail Service Center to Fred and Thelma Leibertz.

The Leibertz family, along with their daughter Gay Lynn, shortened the name to Trail Center and successfully operated the business for several years. Thelma became known for her pies and gift shop. After Fred died, Thelma and Gay Lynn opened a gift shop in the Fitger's building in Duluth.

After selling Trail Service Center, my parents and Floyd decided to start a cabin-building business, using a portion of Floyd's property on Birch Lake. My father also started selling real estate and worked as a desk manager at Lutsen Resort in the winter months. During that time, my parents enjoyed meeting Cindy Nelson, the daughter of the owners of Lutsen. Cindy Nelson competed in three Winter Olympics and won a bronze medal for downhill skiing in Innsbruck. In 1982, she received a silver medal in the World Championships in Austria.

In the late 1960s, my uncle Carl, who still owned property on Poplar Lake, started to draw up plans for another family cabin. He wanted his daughter Carlene and his young grandson to continue to enjoy the Gunflint Trail. Unfortunately, this was not to be. Carl became ill and died in 1969 at the age of sixty-two.

By 1970, Floyd's retirement was in full swing. Even though he lived alone with his golden retriever Ringo, he had many friends in Grand Marais and on the Gunflint Trail. Floyd adored his wilderness life—both in winter and summer. Before there were any groomed, designated

Floyd Soderberg and Ringo.

snowmobile trails, he and my parents used portage trails to travel into Moss Lake, where they ice fished and made coffee in the snow.

Hamms Beer Commercial

During this time, Floyd and his dog Ringo were asked to make a commercial for Hamm's beer. Ever since the 1950s, Hamm's had been making print ads and calendars using photos of lakes and streams near the end of the Gunflint Trail. Their slogan "From the land of sky-blue waters" still resonates today.

According to my mother, a Hamm's commercial featuring Floyd and Ringo was filmed, but, to my knowledge, no one ever saw it. I'm not sure it ever actually aired. Around the same time (1973), Hamm's made its first commercial with a Kodiak bear named Sasha and his trainer Earl Hammond. These commercials became a great marketing success. Though I often wonder if Floyd ever told the Hamm's people about our neighbor, Frenchy, who was known to motor down Birch Lake with his pet bear.

The Dead Sea

Sometime in the 1970s, the Minnesota Department of Natural Resources decided to return Birch Lake to its native state and designate it as

Ralph and Bea Griffis of Chik-wauk Lodge with Earl and Sasha the bear.

a trout lake. I don't think Floyd was very upset about this decision as fishing had been poor for a number of years. In fact, we all began to refer to Birch Lake as the "Dead Sea."

After the lake was poisoned, Floyd took his boat and motored the entire shoreline to see if he could find the remains of one particular fish. Sure enough, he found him—a very old, scarred, large northern pike. It seems that this northern and Floyd had sparred together for many years. Several times Floyd almost brought him into the boat, but at the last minute the fish always got away. As a type of tribute, Floyd hung the old northern's head on his boathouse. I believe Floyd identified with that fish as he passed on a short time later in 1974.

17

The Legacy Continues

As age made the wilderness more limiting, my parents began to spend their winters in Florida, where they purchased a home. However, every summer they would return to Birch Lake and stay in one of Floyd's friends' cabins. They still enjoyed many close friendships: Gene Doody on Birch Lake, Lydia Miller, Emerson and Jeanette Morris on Poplar Lake, Roy and Rose Carlson on Mayhew Lake, Marie and Joseph Simonson on West Pope, and Margaret and Harry Nolan in Grand Marais.

Two years after Floyd's death, Emerson Morris helped my parents build another cabin on Birch Lake. After several renovations by Emerson's artisan son Keith Morris and good friend Bob Johnson of Poplar Lake, that cabin is our home today, holding fifty years of family history.

Cycles of Family and Friends

Over these fifty years, my husband and I have seen our children and grandchildren grow up at Birch Lake. We have also had the privilege of introducing the wilderness to friends and family from other states and countries. It is unbelievable that during this time, we have watched the construction of another twenty-five or more cabins on Birch Lake, and have seen many of these cabin owners come and go.

While the summer months offer our family a wide range of adventure and activity, the winter months have become my favorite. Surrounded by the magic of snow and ice, we experience the seclusion of the wilderness from years past.

Eva's last trip on Saganaga Lake at 86 years old.

Our first Christmas on Birch Lake was celebrated in forty below zero temperatures, with no running water and very meager heat coming from a fireplace and potbelly stove. That year, we hauled buckets of water from the lake during a swirling, white-out blizzard, using a clothesline rope to guide us safely back to the cabin.

When the weather eased, we had a great time riding down the lake on Floyd's old snowmobile, pulling our children behind on a dog sled. We even found a navigable trail that led us through a canopy of snow-laden trees. We were in awe when we passed a family of moose feeding nearby.

As snowmobiles improved and a large network of trails was eventually laid out and groomed, my husband and I explored new routes. While in our sixties, we drove the seventy-mile round trip to Grand Marais in one day. The year we turned eighty, an adventurous friend led us to hidden lakes on snowmobile trails we hadn't seen before.

Today, our family still comes from near and far to celebrate Christmas on Birch Lake. For the last several years, we have added to the celebration by holding a Scandinavian smörgåsborg feast, where local friends bring their favorite foods and join us on Christmas Eve. These lake friends are met at the door with mugs of steaming glögg. Arrowhead Electric added to the festive spirit by lighting a forty-foot Christmas tree on the Gunflint Trail which a small group of Birch Lake residents have tended over the last ten years.

Cycles Within the Forest

A forest never stays the same—there will always be cycles of weather and fire. As a child, I loved the giant pines that lined so many trails and the silence their discarded pine needles created. Even Helen Keller once wrote, "To me a lush carpet of pine needles or spongy grass is more welcome than the most luxurious Persian rug."

Since those years, we have witnessed the July 4,1999, blowdown storm, where ninety-mile-per-hour winds downed millions of trees. More recently, on May 5, 2007, the Ham Lake fire consumed over seventy-five thousand acres in northeast Minnesota and Canada. Thankfully, with time and replanting, we have seen the forest renewed with aspens, spruces, balsams, and jack pines.

George Cleaver.

During the Ham Lake fire, we were living in southern California. I remember watching the news one morning and seeing Sarah Hamilton of Trail Center packing up to evacuate. That week, I was part of a group of artists who were painting vistas from a hilltop at Pepperdine College in Malibu. While I was serenely looking out over the ocean, I received a phone call from a neighbor, telling me that the Ham Lake fire had most likely destroyed our cabin.

Interestingly, I had just read an article that week claiming that if a phone rings during a fire, it means a house is still intact. Immediately, I grabbed my cell phone and dialed our cabin. To my great relief, it rang. Later, we learned that the fire reached as far as Mayhew Lake and then stopped. Birch Lake did not burn.

That fire was devastating and sobering. Since then, many cabin owners have installed sprinkler systems, which were proven to have helped protect cabins during the Ham Lake fire.

Cycles of Wildlife

Throughout the years, I've been thrilled to see a moose rise up out of the water as my husband and I quietly paddled by. I've been enchanted by a hummingbird as it affectionately fluttered its feathers against my outstretched hand. I have admired the stately eagles as they stand guard over our lake, and the persistent turtles as they slowly climb up to our road from the lake, seeking a place to lay their eggs. I've even laughed over a pine martin that broke through our screened-in porch and ate a large section of frozen turkey that I had planned to serve for Christmas dinner.

As with the forest, there is a cycle of wildlife. Although there have been occasional sightings of lynx, bobcats, and mountain lions, the presence of moose, deer, bear, and wolves seems to regularly come and go. Today, I rarely see any evidence of porcupine, which were major pests when I was a child. I also don't remember any ticks as a child. However, the presence of pesky squirrels, mice, leeches, black flies, and mosquitoes always remains the same.

It's worth noting that the ticks that are believed to be impacting our moose population today were also causing harm years ago. Old-timer Billy Needham, in an interview, was quoted as saying that shortly after he arrived on the Gunflint Trail, the moose population began dying off. He commented that the moose were full of big ticks, and they were dead all over the woods.

One night, several years ago, a five-hundred-pound malicious bear that had already blown apart an oil drum trap tried to break through our cabin door.

It was spring, and I had just arrived from Barrington, Illinois, with my teenage son and mother, Eva, now in her late eighties. As I drove down the road, a neighbor stopped our car and warned us that a dangerous bear had been at his cabin every night. As he stood, armed with his rifle, I couldn't help but see the look of frustration and alarm in his eyes. I also couldn't help but see a large window shutter hanging askew off his cabin window.

At about ten o'clock that night, I heard gunfire, signaling the bear was back. Not long after, my mother's small dog started to yap at our one and only door. During the commotion, while my mother and son slept, I weighed our options. Although I found my grandfather's old rifle, there were no shells. I picked up the telephone and realized it was still disconnected from the winter. I then realized that if the bear broke through the door, our only escape would be to jump off a second-story deck.

Thankfully, after about ten minutes, the bear left. When he came back the next night, my son and I blocked the door with our large fireplace wood box. A day or two later, my husband arrived and laughed when I told him about the bear. But when he saw the bear's muddy snout and giant paw prints on our door, he gained a great amount of respect. Later, we were relieved to hear that the bear had been killed.

18

Reflections

In 1885, my mother's family, the Soderbergs, started their trek on Minnesota's wilderness trails. By the 1920s, they had reached the Gunflint Trail—the greatest trail of all. Over the next one hundred years, I believe the Soderberg family left a lasting mark on this trail, and their footprints can still be traced today.

My motive for documenting the Soderberg family saga has been twofold. First, to praise the wonders of Minnesota and its preservation of the wilderness. And second, to honor all the men and women who had the courage to brave this wilderness in order to carve out new lives. I believe there are many simple, unknown families who should not be forgotten today; they deserve a note of praise. May my family symbolically represent those.

A Bridge

I hope my Minnesota memories can somehow act as a bridge between the old and the new. I hope these memories will reinforce how valuable the wilderness is to the human spirit and Earth itself. I hope this bridge of memories will help each of us to rethink what new forms of wilderness safeguards might be needed as we head into the future.

When the BWCAW acquired wilderness status in the 1970s, there were concerns that the new limits imposed upon the Boundary Waters would deter the neophyte vacationer, or someone who was older or handicapped. Today, the presence of technology raises some opposite concerns. As we have learned, technology is not subject to boundaries—it can cross any line.

New Trail Blazers

I have lived on this land without electric lines and telephone lines. Even though I thought it was wonderful progress when our cabin first shared a phone line with a neighbor, I now ponder how broadband and cellphones will change the atmosphere of this protected wilderness.

COVID-19, along with the advancements of technology, has made working from home now part of the norm. It has also given people an opportunity to move to more remote, unique places. As I look ahead, I question whether this "ease of access" created by computer chips and Zoom will somehow threaten what we all really seek—an untouched land of natural beauty, a separation from civilization, and being one with all things wild.

A bridge can only extend halfway. May this little bridge of history both welcome and caution new trailblazers as they step onto Minnesota's precious, time-honored trails.

Endnotes

1. Dag Blanck, "Swedish Immigration to the U.S./Svensk invandring till USA," *Minnesota Historical Society*, https://www.mnhs.org/newpapers/swedishamerican-migration.

2. Hans Högman, "Tutorial 11a: How to Research Conscripts, 1800s, Sweden," *Military Hans Högman*, www.hhogman.se.

3. "Larsonw," Family Search (blog), January 26, 2011, https://www.familysearch.org/en/blog/the-unique-names-of-swedish-soldiers.

4. G. Fröberg Morris, "Soldier Farm: 'Torps in Sweden'," *The Swedish Genealogy Guide*, last modified May 20, 2015, Swedishgenealogyguide.com/archives/329.

5. Hans Högman, "The Old Agricultural Society and its People—Sweden," *History Hans Högman*, Dec, 2022, hhogman.se/agricultural-society.htm.

6. Ulf Beijbom, "Sillgatan—The Emigrant Path through Gothenborg," *Göteborgs Regionens Släktforskare*, https//www.genealogigbg.se/.

7. "Emigrant Routes to The Promised Land in America," *New Sweden Cultural Heritage Society*,   www.newsweden.org/lib/doc/culture/Emigration Routes.pdf.

8. "Overview and History: Ellis Island," *The Statue of Liberty—Ellis Island Foundation, Inc.*, https://www.statueofliberty.org.

9. "History," *Village of Grantsburg*, Wisconsin, http://www.grantsburgwi.com/ learn-about-grantsburgs-history.html.

10. "With a Bang: Not a Whimper—The Winter of 1887—1888," *Minnesota State Climatology Office*, Climateapps.dnr.statement.

11. Jennifer Yocum-Stans, "A History of the Sandstone Quarry: Part I," *Pine County News*, Jennifer, last modified June 1, 2022.

12. Muriel Langseth (Ed.), *Sandstone, the Quarry City*, (Dallas: Taylor Publishing Company, 1989).

13.   "Minnesota History of the Land" (video), *Bell Museum, History Channel*, three episodes, 2013.

14. "Forest Conservation," *Minnesota Historical Society*, Forest History Center, www.mnhs.org.

15. Leif Enger, "A History of Timbering in Minnesota," *MPR*, November 16, 1998.

16. Evadene Burris Swanson, "The Use and Conservation of Minnesota Wilderness 1850—1900, II The Fur Trade in Minnesota 1850—1900," June, 1940.

17. Earl J. Foster and Amy Troolin, "Image of America," *Northern Pine County*.

18. Hinckley Fire Museum, "Hinckley Fire 1894," YouTube video, 11:46, September 11, 2020, https://www.youtube.com/watch?v=5K8cSRfdw-I.

19. *City of Hinckley*.

20. Gudmund Emanuel Akermark and William Johnson, *Eld-cyklonen or Hinckley Fire*, (Pine County Historical Society, January 1, 1976, reprinted by the Hinckley Fire Museum), p. 66.

21. With the permission of the Pine County Historical Society. Originally translated from Swedish in 1895.

22. Websites: history for Clearwater Lodge, Old Northwoods Lodge, Gunflint Lodge, Nor'wester Lodge, Hungry Jack Lodge, Trail Center Lodge.

23. Chik-Wauk Museum's chronological history of roads, events, and places.

24. William C. Boissenin, "Civilian Conservation Corps Along the Gunflint Trail," prepared for the Gunflint Trail Historical Society, Chik-Wauk Museum library collection, March 10, 2021.

25. Carlene Soderberg, "Memories of the Gunflint Trail," Chik-Wauk Museum library collection.

26. "Boundary Waters Canoe Area Wilderness," *USDA Forest Service*, https:/www.fs.usda.gov/rearea/superior/recrea/precid=84168.

27. Steve Blumke, "Aspen Annie," Gunflint Trail Historical Society talk, August 8, 2022.

28. "Haffner Mystery Still Unsolved," *Cook County News Herald*, October 27, 1949.

29. "Famous Visitors," *Lutsen*.

30. "Tommy Banks Stories or the Minneapolis' Mob Gunflint Connection," *The EDGE: Dirt from the Yurt and other Chatter from the Edge of the Boundary Waters* (blog), July 16, 2005, http://boundarycountry.blogspot.com/.

31. "Organized Crime on the North Shore," *Exploring the North Shore with Joe and Jaye*, 113, https://exploringnorthshore.com/organized-crime/.

32. Chuck Viren, "Sky-Blue Waters, Bears and Beer," *Northern Wilds: For the Love of the North*, January 29, 2018, https://northernwilds.com/sky-blue-waters-bear-beer.

About the Author

Joyce Cleaver Leddy is Eva Soderberg (Cleaver)'s daughter. Joyce has spent eighty-three years visiting the Gunflint Trail. Today, Joyce's two favorite things are still kayaking and snowshoeing. Although Joyce and her husband Tom have lived in California, Illinois, Texas, and France, they now make their home on Birch Lake and Grand Marais, Minnesota.

Joyce worked for her church for many years, which led to writing and public speaking. She is an artist, and her paintings can be found in public and private collections.

The Leddy's two children, Tom and Erin, along with their two grand-daughters, Reilly and Bryn, continue the Soderberg tradition in loving the Gunflint Trail and embracing the Minnesota wilderness.